Compressing the Product Development Cycle From Research to Marketplace

Bernard N. Slade

amacom
American Management Association
New York . Atlanta . Boston . Chicago . Kansas City . San Francisco . Washington, D.C.
Brussels . Toronto . Mexico City

This book is available at a special
discount when ordered in bulk quantities.
For information, contact Special Sales Department,
AMACOM, a division of American Management Association,
135 West 50th Street, New York, NY 10020.

This publication is designed to provide accurate and authoritative
information in regard to the subject matter covered. It is sold with the
understanding that the publisher is not engaged in rendering legal,
accounting, or other professional service. If legal advice or other
expert assistance is required, the services of a competent professional
person should be sought.

MB

Library of Congress-Cataloging-in-Publication Data
Slade, Bernard N.
    Compressing the product development cycle / Bernard N. Slade.
      p.   cm.
    Includes bibliographical references and index.
    ISBN 0–8144–5006–7
      1. New products——United States.   2. Product management.
  I. Title.
  HF5415.153.S58   1993
  658.5′75——dc20   92–27375
                                                  CIP

Printing number

10 9 8 7 6 5 4 3 2 1

To
Margot, Steven, Eric, and Joy

Table of Contents

Preface   *vii*

Chapter 1   Introduction   1
Chapter 2   Technology and the Integrated Company   7
Chapter 3   The Product Cycle: Critical Gears That Drive It   22
Chapter 4   Strategic Direction: Management of Change and Risk   39
Chapter 5   Research: The Technical Foundation   55
Chapter 6   Integrated Product and Process Design   70
Chapter 7   The Prototype: The Product Integrator   92
Chapter 8   The Supplier: A Partner in the Product Cycle   111
Chapter 9   Investments: When Do You Make Them?   129
Chapter 10   Learning: The Key to Shorter Product Cycles   138
Chapter 11   Managing the Critical Path   155
Chapter 12   Epilogue   164

Appendix A   U.S. Industry and Competition: How Good—or Bad—Are We?   169

Appendix **B**   Case Studies: How Different
Companies Manage the Product
Cycle   186

               Bibliography   *209*

               Index   *211*

Preface

This book is about the most serious problem crippling U.S. industrial leadership—our difficulty in expediting the movement of new technology and product concepts from invention to the customer. Despite the abundance of valuable research and writings on many aspects of this subject, the solution to this perplexing problem continues to evade us.

I have written this book because I believe I bring a unique perspective to the subject—one that comes out of my long and varied industrial experience. As any author of a professional or technical book will attest, it takes at least two years and possibly many more to write one. In many respects, it took me forty-four years. For almost the entire period beginning shortly after the end of World War II until today, I have been privileged to participate directly in an exciting age of American industrial expansion and leadership, an era unequalled in the history of the world. My experience has spanned almost the entire spectrum of the corporation; it includes thirty-six years in research, development, manufacturing, and corporate management, supplemented by an additional eight years of consulting in a number of industries.

I have personally invented, designed, and moved new products from the laboratory to the factory floor. I have coped with more than my share of sixteen-hour days, seven days a week, to defuse crises, expedite product designs, break production bottlenecks, and struggle to meet back-breaking schedules. With many successes, punctuated by some serious problems, and even a few failures, I have learned a great deal about what will and will not work. The best teacher is experience, and all of these experiences have given me a rare vantage point from which to view the problems of the product cycle and propose methods to solve them. Consequently, with all of my industrial battle scars, I believe I bring knowledge and insights that are different from those of others who have studied and written about this subject.

But I did not write this book alone. Most professional and management books carry the names of only one or two authors. Yet behind those names are countless contributors who were vital to the completion and success of the books. In fact, it is virtually impossible to list the names of everyone who, in varying degrees, made this work possible. But there are many who deserve particular acknowledgment because of the importance of their assistance.

First, I am greatly indebted to the following people from Gemini Consulting: Professor Edward Harris reviewed most of the book and made indispensable contributions to its clarity and organization; Dana Cahoon very effectively translated ideas and data into the illustrations; Pat Morey made invaluable contributions to the description of the product development process; Kevin Barry, Lance Totten, and other members of the Gemini Technical Center did an outstanding job of researching countless sources of information; Margaret Nicholson did an excellent job in preparing the final draft for submission to the publisher.

I am very grateful for the support I received from David Teiger and Dan Valentino of Gemini Consulting, as well as for the special interest and encouragement of David Hewitt of Gemini.

I would like to thank Arthur Schneiderman of Analog Devices, Heinz Piorunneck of Burndy, Dr. William Prindle of Corning, Dr. James Carnes of the David Sarnoff Research Center, Henning Kornbrekke of Stanley Magic-Door, Robert Crandall of Kodak, Dr. Michael Ervin of DuPont, Dr. David Milligan of Abbott Laboratories, and Glenn Dreeson of Caterpillar for the invaluable and stimulating discussions that led to the case studies. I would also like to express my appreciation to Alfred Baker of Thomson Consumer Electronics, Patrick McKeown, and Ralph Tileston for valuable insights into their respective industries.

Special thanks are due Professor John Dixon of the University of Massachusetts and Professor Stephen Rosenthal of

Boston University for their thorough and thoughtful reviews of many of the key chapters. Their recommendations for changes greatly strengthened the book.

I want to thank Raj Mohindra, coauthor of my first book, *Winning the Productivity Race,* for providing me with the impetus for writing this one, as well as for his views concerning many of the ideas and issues I discuss.

My editor, Myles Thompson, gave me valuable guidance and support, for which I am very grateful.

And finally, I am deeply indebted to my wife, Margot, who did far more than survive this long ordeal and provide the obligatory spousal tolerance and moral support. She was a very effective sounding board and critic throughout the entire writing process. Furthermore, she edited the entire book, and her work was an essential ingredient toward its completion.

Chapter 1

Introduction

The greatest roadblock to U.S. worldwide industrial leadership continues to be the excessive length of the cycle from product concept to marketplace. Despite Herculean efforts by many companies to bring new products and technologies to market faster, this serious problem still defies solution.

Where do we look for a cure? Is our declining competitiveness caused by such widely publicized problems as a short-term investment psychology, fiscal policies and a tax structure that discourage capital formation and entrepreneurship, and an inferior educational system? Or are these perceived barriers only smoke screens for poor management and serious internal problems within U.S. corporations? The increasingly prevalent opinion, both in academic circles and in U.S. industry itself, is that although these factors handicap our ability to compete, the major barriers to competitiveness exist within corporations themselves. And the most serious roadblock is the excessive time necessary to move a new product to the customer. Any top executive of a company engaged in a competitive industry will tell you that his most serious problem is speed to market. In this book I explore this problem, the principal reasons for it, and the actions corporate America must take to solve it.

Since the early 1980s, this issue has been extensively and intensively scrutinized and publicized, and the debate on this question continues without letup. For example, two recently published studies from academia have contributed to our knowledge of this subject by comparing the Japanese and U.S. automobile industries, with an emphasis on the product development cycle.[1] My treatment of the problem, however, differs significantly from most others.

Most published works in this field concentrate primarily on specific aspects of the product cycle, such as the interaction between design and manufacturing engineers or the efficiency of manufacturing operations after the product has reached the factory floor. They tend to focus primarily on products composed of mechanical assemblies and to center on individual organizational processes: simultaneous engineering, interdisciplinary teams, design for manufacturability, and technical tools such as statistical process control or design-for-assembly techniques. As important as these specific issues may be to the problem of long cycles, they are not, by themselves, the key to a lasting solution. All these methods and tools constitute only a small part of a much broader range of critical factors.

The key to shorter cycles lies in understanding these critical elements and how they must be managed—not as a series of independent pieces, but as a totally integrated whole. To find the ultimate solution to the problem of long cycles, we need to reach back much further to the very points of origin of any new product: the research laboratory and customer needs. In addition, we must recognize that the mechanical character of products is rapidly being supplemented and in some cases totally replaced by a complex assembly of components based on the science of materials and the physical sciences.

During the preparation of this book, I checked my ideas with faculty members of leading graduate schools as well as key executives in industry. In Appendix A, I review the results of comprehensive interviews I conducted with many of America's top academic authorities on U.S. industrial competitiveness and of detailed surveys of company executives. I carried out this work in conjunction with my colleagues at

---

1. Kim B. Clark and Takahiro Fujimoto, *Product Development Performance: Strategy, Organization, and Management in the World Auto Industry* (Boston: Harvard Business School Press, 1991); James P. Womack, Daniel T. Jones, and Daniel Roos, *The Machine That Changed the World* (New York: Rawson Associates, 1990).

Gemini Consulting; the American Management Association assisted in the executive surveys. One of the most notable results of these studies was the general agreement that although many external societal and governmental factors act as serious handicaps to U.S. industry, the primary causes of our industrial problems are within the companies themselves.

In order to test the applicability of many of the issues covered in the book, I interviewed a cross section of executives from leading companies in a range of industries to determine how they executed their product cycles as well as to discover the strengths and weaknesses in their respective approaches. Appendix B contains case studies resulting from these interviews, which are also referred to in other chapters. These surveys and discussions gave me the courage of my convictions and backed them up with a wide range of practical experience from several industries.

What This Book Does and Does Not Do

This book is not a cookbook—there are no recipes or detailed lists of ingredients for product development. Nor is it a handbook or an instruction manual. A useful checklist of simple solutions to the problems of the product cycle will not be found here or anywhere else. The management of technology and new products through the arduous and perilous labyrinth of the product cycle will not yield to such easy solutions.

Since the early 1970s, U.S. industry has been frantically searching, with little success, for quick and easy answers to our competition problem. The remedies are not simple. The solution to the problem of long development cycles requires significant change in management's mind-set, skills, and behavior, and even in the structure of U.S. corporations. My objective is to explore the most critical factors that drive the product cycle, why they are important, what we must understand about them, and the steps companies must take to meet this demand for change.

In their book *Competing Against Time,* Stalk and Hout state:

Today's innovation is time based competition. Demanding executives at aggressive companies are altering their measures of performance from competitive costs and quality to competitive costs, quality and responsiveness. Time based competitors are offering greater varieties of products and services, at lower costs and in less time than their more pedestrian competitors.[2]

Arguably the most important time-based factor that can spell the difference between leading companies and their "pedestrian competitors" is the speed of the development cycle. But time, cost, and quality alone are not the only criteria of success. A shorter time to market must be accompanied by:

• Wide acceptability of the product in the marketplace
• The advancement of technology and product performance
• An increasing success rate of new product programs

The competitive challenge any company faces is to achieve *all* these objectives faster than its competitors. Consequently, when I discuss the means of shortening the product cycle, the implication is that a combination of all these criteria is also being achieved.

My primary tenet is that the basic reason for long development cycles is the existence of an intricate and interrelated *combination* of several deeply rooted organizational, behavioral, and technical weaknesses in U.S. industrial corporations that act as serious barriers to shorter product development cycles and higher-quality products. They cannot be removed by piecemeal efforts to eliminate each one of them individually and independently from the others. Nor will they be eliminated by chasing one panacea after another in the quest for a miracle cure. This book defines these weaknesses and proposes how to overcome them.

2. George Stalk, Jr., and Thomas M. Hout, *Competing Against Time: How Time-Based Competition Is Reshaping Global Markets* (New York: Free Press, a Division of Macmillan, Inc., 1990), p. 1. Used with permission of the publisher.

Unfortunately, these weaknesses occur precisely in those areas of the management process that require the most strength, the highest management priority and concentration, and the application of the greatest skills. Yet all too often they are given the least management emphasis. This book explores why these areas have the greatest leverage for achieving success, why U.S. industry is putting too little emphasis on them, and what steps company management must take to strengthen them. Specifically, I demonstrate that:

• Advancing technology is the principal factor forcing companies to make major organizational changes toward integrating their operations. I discuss what integration really means and list some of the measures that must be taken to achieve it.

• Today's products are becoming increasingly dependent on mastery of the physical sciences, which must serve as the foundation for success of the product cycle. Some of the most difficult design and production problems, which are major factors in causing long product cycles, occur because companies put too little emphasis on gaining that fundamental knowledge.

• There is a "critical path" of key elements or segments of the cycle that have the greatest leverage in reducing its length and improving product quality. Although many of these elements have been widely discussed, some are given far too low a priority, and they have many subtle but highly important aspects that must be understood if companies are to implement them successfully.

• Every new product contains a small number of critical, novel, and advanced components, design features, or manufacturing processes that are of overriding importance to its ultimate performance. The degree of emphasis given to these vital parts of the product, and the way the critical elements of the cycle are applied to develop them, will determine the ultimate success of the program.

• Certain personnel and organizational practices greatly handicap the product cycle and stifle the learning process essential to its success. I show why changes in these practices should contribute to faster learning and shorter product cycles.

Two other issues are of major importance in achieving a shorter development cycle. These ingredients of success have become verities with which no one could possibly disagree, but they have been discussed far more than they have been practiced. The first is the need for corporate integration. The second is the necessity for top management involvement to make the product cycle work. Both of these requirements demand significant change in organizational and management behavior. Neither can be achieved easily, but they are necessary elements in the quest for shorter cycles. In this book, I explore these issues in considerable depth and provide additional insight into what these objectives really mean, why they are so important, and steps that must be taken to make them work.

Chapter 2

Technology and the Integrated Company

One of the most astonishing features of life today is the quickening pace of innovation. The rate of change in product performance and technological sophistication is staggering. Consider the following developments:

* From 1965 to 1990, the density of bits in magnetic recording has grown from 200,000 to 100 million per square inch.

* In 1974, the fuel efficiency of the average new domestic passenger car was only 13.7 miles per gallon. A mere fifteen years later, it had more than doubled, rising to 28 miles per gallon.

* Fiber-optic cables can now transmit information over telephone lines at the rate of billions of bits per second compared to 64,000 bits per second over copper wire; new techniques for beaming signals through fibers may boost these levels another thousand times.

* With the use of a refinement technique for producing pure silicon dioxide, the transparency of glass has been increased 10,000 times since the 1960s.

* After twenty-five years of development, DuPont has produced a fabric called Kevlar, which is five times stronger than steel.

* From 1970 to 1990, the density of circuits on a silicon chip has jumped from 1,000 to 8 million.

These advances in technology have dramatically increased the power of computers, revolutionized telecommunications, reduced the cost of automobile travel, and decreased air pollution. Yet, as the rate of technological progress continues to escalate, so does the complexity of the products our corporations manufacture. This spiraling complexity, in turn, has a profound influence on how companies are managed. Although there have been stunning advances in products and technology since the early 1960s, our methods of managing their development and manufacture have not kept pace. As a result, many companies are not realizing the full potential that modern technology holds for enhancing their competitive advantage. The mismatch between the new technology and the old methods of management is perhaps the most serious issue facing U.S. business today.

The Impact of Technological Progress on the Product Cycle

Before we discuss the steps companies must take to transform their businesses, we need to take a closer look at the nature of these technological advances and their impact on the product cycle. Let us start by clarifying what we mean by *technology*. The *American Heritage Dictionary of the English Language* gives the following definition:

> the application of science, especially to industrial or commercial objectives; the entire body of methods and materials used to achieve such objectives.

In other words, technology is a vital link in applying science to the ultimate product. For example, iron is converted to tough stainless steel for knives and razor blades by adding nickel, molybdenum, tungsten, or chromium. Raw silicon is converted to integrated circuits by embedding metals and depositing circuit components with methods such as diffusion, evaporation, and photolithography. Consequently, the application of technology becomes a major factor in making the transition from scientific knowledge to new products, and it has a profound influence on every step of the cycle to convert that knowledge to a product.

Every product from paper clips to laser-guided missiles uses some level of technology. A pair of scissors contains a relatively low technology content, a food processor represents a much higher level, and a supercomputer is an example of one of the most advanced and sophisticated uses of technology. Obviously those products that require only a low level of technology are relatively simple to manufacture. But as the level of technology employed by a company increases, the management systems required to translate technology into products become more complex and challenging. This brings us to the concept of the product cycle. Every product must travel a sequence of steps that form a path from the research laboratory to the marketplace. At each step along the way, a new product encounters the risk of failure. As the level of technology increases, this path becomes longer and the number of risks encountered multiplies. This path is called the product cycle.

In the 1950s, the product cycle was much shorter and contained fewer risks than it does today. Lawn mowers, machine tools, and home appliances were made up of relatively few mechanical and electrical parts. Even the most sophisticated products such as calculators or automobiles were relatively simple to assemble and manufacture compared to their counterparts of today. The road these products traveled to reach the market was fairly straightforward and easy to follow. The design engineer had little difficulty describing the process of assembling products to the manufacturer and the external suppliers. The manufacturer found it easy to decipher and copy the design specifications and to prepare for mass production. If any parts turned out to be defective, they could be reworked or replaced during the assembly process. Under these conditions the yield of good products was virtually 100 percent.

The length of the product cycle was primarily dependent on what happened on the factory floor. The linchpin of the system was the efficiency of the individual factory worker. Bottlenecks and high work-in-progress inventories might have threatened to slow down the product on its journey to the marketplace, but these problems could be solved by improving worker and equipment productivity, adding workers, paying overtime, and managing aggressively.

The introduction of higher technology in the last thirty years has changed the product cycle almost beyond recognition. What used to be a short path has now become a long, complex journey. For example, the process of manufacturing the semiconductor integrated circuit, the magnetic disk, and the electronic package each requires has as many as several hundred discrete steps. The chain of operations in the production process has acquired dozens of new links. The physical dimensions of products have become microscopic, and there are many new interrelationships between chemical and metallurgical processes. In short, these and a host of other factors have radically altered the relationship between design and manufacturing engineers, between the research scientist and the marketing strategist. Furthermore, one look at the appliances in our kitchens, the dashboards of our automobiles, or the controls of today's machine tools shows that this dramatic increase of complexity extends well beyond the integrated circuit, the magnetic disk, or the computer.

The new realities of manufacturing require a new and more intensive form of collaboration among all components in the product cycle. The product designer must work closely with the manufacturing engineer to ensure that the company can manufacture the product at low cost and with high quality. The research scientist must be involved at critical stages so that there is a strong technical foundation underlying all work done to design and manufacture the product. This basic technical knowledge of the physical sciences is a prerequisite to the design and development process. And the participation of the marketing strategist is essential if the product is to meet the needs of the marketplace.

The heightened level of collaboration necessitated by advances in technology is driving the trend toward teamwork and greater corporate integration. The manufacturing plant of today has become a highly interactive system of skilled labor, new materials, sophisticated production equipment and processes, computerized information systems, and electronic controls. Add to this an intricate series of chemical, metallurgical, mechanical, electrical, and optical processes. Individually and collectively, these elements not only interact with but influence the actual design of a product. The result of these developments is that companies can no longer approach product design and manufacturing as two separate processes. Given the complex interrelationships among all phases of the product cycle, companies must now design products and the means for manufacturing those products simultaneously and interactively. In addition, both product design and manufacturing must be solidly based on a rigorously developed technical foundation.

As the rate of technological change accelerates, the traditional methods of managing industrial enterprises are becoming obsolete. What worked in an era of relative simplicity is ceasing to be relevant to the demands of our era of high technology. To succeed in a rapidly changing environment, companies must promote tightly linked integration of all aspects of the business.

How the Integrated System Works

We can describe almost any product manufactured by industry as a system of interactive parts. Take, for example, the automobile. The engine, the transmission, the fuel system, the lubricants, and the microprocessor controls are all highly interdependent. Like the brain, heart, lungs, and arteries in the human body, one cannot function without all the others. Nor can we design any single part and accurately test its performance in isolation from the rest of the system. Yet each one of the major components of the automobile is itself a system with its own set of interacting parts. For instance, the engine contains a block, pistons, rings, valves, lubrication, distribution, and many other interlocking pieces.

But it is not enough to attach a state-of-the-art engine to a superior fuel system and a first-rate transmission. The entire automobile must be designed as a whole. This means that the quality of the interaction between the parts is just as important as the quality of the individual pieces. As automotive technology advances, and the number of parts and their interrelationships multiply, the overall impact of these interrelationships on the automobile's performance increases enormously.

Let us look at another example. As noted earlier, the density of the silicon chip has grown at an exponential rate ever since the invention of the integrated circuit in the early 1960s. The strides made in this technology are so immense that the features on the silicon surface are now measured in submicron dimensions. Allowable contamination has been reduced to submicroscopic levels. Hundreds of individual process operations are required to manufacture a silicon chip.

The design of the chip and these production operations together constitute a highly interactive system (Figure 2-1). The origin of the system is the objectives and specifications that are determined by marketing and engineering. These objectives determine the chip density and the dimensions of the circuits to be built into the chip. The design, density, and dimensions of the chip in turn determine the number of process operations required. Finally, the number and nature of these process operations determine the type and design of the production equipment and the level of precision the equipment must attain to perform these processes. All these elements of the design and process will influence the future shape of the production facility, the work flow, parts logistics, plant environment, methods of chemical disposal, and methods for ensuring employee safety.

The entire system must function as a unified integrated whole, not as a series of independent, unrelated events. Like a chain, the system is no stronger than its weakest link. Every single part of the system, no matter how minor, must consequently receive careful scrutiny. Even the most sophisticated and complex products can fail if just one simple part is defective. The tragedy of the U.S. space shuttle *Challenger* reminded everyone of the importance of this lesson. Here the poor design of a simple rubber O ring on the rocket booster cost the lives of seven astronauts.

Adjusting to Technological Change

This increase in the complexity of products and their behavior as integrated systems is made possible by advances in tech-

Figure 2-1. Design system for integrated chip.

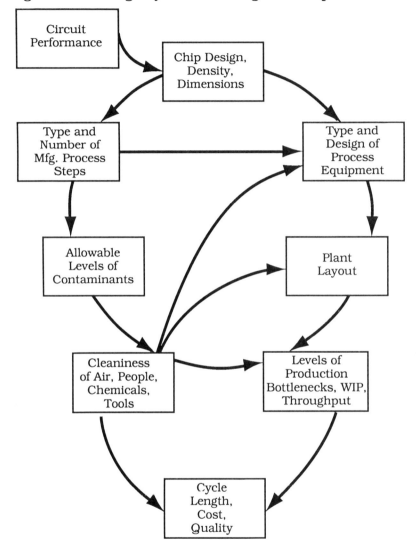

nology. One of the major factors driving these advances is worldwide competition. As national economies grow stronger, customer appetites expand, and trade barriers fall, these competitive pressures intensify, forcing every industry to advance its technology in the search for better products. In the past, when technological developments moved ahead more slowly, companies could introduce product changes at a slower pace.

Today, technology and product advance are accelerating under this intensive competitive pressure. These rapid advances create moving targets for companies: Once they confront and master one challenge, they must rapidly change and adapt to the next. However, there are different degrees of change, and the methods used to manage the product cycle will vary, depending on the magnitude of the change. For purposes of this book, change can be classified into three different categories:

1. Evolutionary
2. Incremental
3. Revolutionary

Evolutionary change is characterized by small advances from product to product. These advances marginally improve cost and performance. The cycle time for implementing them is relatively short, and the technical, management, and manufacturing challenges are quite modest. For example, many of the appliances in our kitchens are characterized by frequent but small enhancements.

Incremental change involves more significant advances that create more sizable improvements in cost and performance. They may not involve major differences in technology, but they incorporate significant new design features and manufacturing processes. The management challenge in developing such products is much greater and the problems are far more complex. The automobile industry is an example of one in which there are annual incremental changes of varying sizes.

Revolutionary change is characterized by major shifts in technology, new materials, radical dimensional reductions, far more precision, much greater component and subsystem complexity, and, in some cases, completely new principles of operation. This type of change cannot be realized in the marketplace in one step; it may take years or even decades before products that use these new technologies can be commercialized. Examples are the advances from piston to jet engines, steam to diesel engines, and vacuum tubes to transistors.

In an analysis of technology change, Anderson and Tushman of Cornell and Columbia universities, have proposed a model that describes the revolutionary change or, as they label it, "technological breakthrough."[1] They suggest that at the time of each breakthrough, a major discontinuity exists between the old technology and the new one. This period of discontinuity is followed by two major phases of the development of this new technology. The first phase consists of an era of intense competition, instability, and ferment. After that phase subsides, a "single dominant design" emerges in industry, shared by all companies that incorporate that technology in their products. At that point, a lengthy period of "incremental technical progress" begins and continues until the next discontinuity arrives. Let us look at these two phases in more detail.

The Instability, Ferment, and Chaos Phase

In his book on innovation, Foster portrays the discontinuity as the gap between two S curves (see Figure 2-2a later in this chapter).[2] The S curve describes the degree of improvement in the performance of a technology as its development progresses. As the curve for one technology begins to reach a point at which it matures and approaches its limits of performance, a new technology is invented that further extends those limits. Foster describes the discontinuity as a period of "chaos. . . . Companies that have learned how to cross technological discontinuities escaped this trap. . . . A change in technology may not be the leading number-one killer, but it certainly is among the leading causes of corporate ill health."[3] A prime example of a major discontinuity and its ill effects on some leading electronics companies was the dramatic shift from vacuum tubes to transistors. The switch to the transistor represented a gigantic technological discontinuity because it used completely new materials and a totally different mechanism of operation.

1. Philip Anderson and Michael L. Tushman, *Technological Discontinuities and Dominant Designs: A Cyclical Model of Technological Change* (Ithaca, N.Y.: Cornell University, 1990).
2. Richard Foster, *Innovation* (New York: Summit Books, 1986).
3. Foster, *Innovation,* pp. 103, 116.

When the Bell Telephone Laboratories announced the invention of the transistor in 1948, the Radio Corporation of America was the titan of the vacuum tube industry. It possessed a strong research laboratory and a dominant position in the electronic component market. But it never gained an important position in the transistor or integrated circuit era. Many other manufacturers of vacuum tubes, industry giants such as General Electric, Sylvania, and Westinghouse, never became major contenders in the blossoming new industry either. Replacing all these old-line tube companies as the leaders of the burgeoning new field were many new, entrepreneurial, and highly innovative companies such as Texas Instruments, National Semiconductor, and Intel. The fact that all the leaders in vacuum tubes failed to become major players in this new era, and the fact that the companies that succeeded had never manufactured a single vacuum tube, may be no coincidence. The old-line tube companies did not have the vision, the flexibility, or a sufficient understanding of the massive changes this new era demanded. They never made the radical shifts in market strategy, management practices, and technical skills needed to cope with the transition to semiconductors. In fact, in the ferment that followed the invention of the transistor, the vacuum tube industry never successfully bridged the discontinuity to semiconductor technology.

The Dominant Design and Incremental Advance Phase

The second stage of the Anderson and Tushman model, after ferment is replaced by more stability, is an era in which most companies in an industry converge on a single dominant design. This design goes through an extended period of incremental improvements that continue for the life of the technology. Practically every major invention has passed through this phase, which can last decades or even centuries.

The internal combustion engine of today, invented in the middle of the nineteenth century, was built on incremental advances. No overnight revolution created the high-compression engine of the superpowered luxury machine or the low fuel consumption of the subcompact car. This technology has been characterized by slow but steady increments toward higher and higher performance. Kevlar, the fiber that is five times stronger than steel, was a major advance in technology, but it took DuPont twenty-five years of development before the product could be commercialized.

The history of the silicon chip industry is another example of the incremental nature of technological advancement. The seeds of the integrated circuit chip of today were sown in 1948 with the invention of the transistor. The first silicon transistors were available for commercial use in the late 1950s. The integrated circuit chip began to appear in the early 1960s. The next twenty years were characterized by a constant stream of incremental advances that continually increased the density of circuits on the silicon chip by a factor of four every three or four years. Although these density increases could be described as incremental, they involved changes in processes and design features that were substantial in magnitude, and each of these changes created a discontinuity with the older process.

To achieve these increases, a process known as photolithography was used to deposit the microscopic-size circuits onto the silicon chip. In order to keep pace with the increasing number of circuits and their decreasing size, the technology of photolithography itself had to pass through five successive generations of major incremental advances. The first process was known as contact printing, followed by proximity printers, scanning projection aligners, and two generations of step and repeat aligners.

In another study of product innovation, Henderson and Clark of MIT and Harvard analyzed the performance of the major manufacturers of photolithographic equipment and the role each played in the development of each of these five generations of equipment. They discovered that each of these generations was dominated by a *different* company (Table 2-1). Cobilt dominated the contact printer market, but the next generation of proximity printers was led by Canon. The following three generations were dominated by Perkin-Elmer, GCA, and Nikon, in that order. No company was able to translate its success in one generation into success in the

Table 2-1.

| | Share of Deflated Cumulative Sales (%) 1962–1986 | | | | |
| | | | | Step and Repeat | |
	Contact	Proximity	Scanners	1st	2nd
Cobilt	44		<1		
Kaspar	17	8		7	
Canon		67	21	9	
Perkin-Elmer			78	10	<1
GCA				55	12
Nikon					70
TOTAL	61	75	99+	81	82+

Source: Rebecca M. Henderson and Kim B. Clark, "Architectural Innovation: The Reconfiguration of Existing Product Technologies and the Failure of Established Firms," *Administrative Science Quarterly,* 35, no. 1 (March 1990). Reprinted by permission of *Administrative Science Quarterly.* Copyright 1990 by Cornell University.

next. Not one of them was able to move through the technological discontinuity from one generation to the next successfully.

Why, despite their experience in photolithographic technology, knowledge of the industry and its markets, and all the skills they had acquired, did each company fail as it tried to make the transition to the next generation? Henderson and Clark state that "our analysis of the industry's history suggests that a reliance on architectural knowledge derived from experience with the previous generation blinded the incumbent firms to critical aspects of the new technology."[4]

When a company moves through a discontinuity, the pat-

4. Rebecca M. Henderson and Kim B. Clark, "Architectural Innovation: The Reconfiguration of Existing Product Technologies and the Failure of Established Firms," *Administrative Science Quarterly* 35, no. 1 (March 1990), p. 24. By permission of *Administrative Science Quarterly,* Copyright 1990 by Cornell University.

terns established by a technology or product are not necessarily transferable to the next generation. Much of the knowledge and experience gained with the older product generation becomes obsolete. Surprisingly, this experience in the photolithographic industry in many ways mirrors the fall of the vacuum tube companies from industry leadership.

Keeping Up With Technological Change

Technological breakthroughs are the most visible and dramatic discontinuities that drive the pace of industry. But in reality, there is a discontinuity in every incremental product, process, and technological advance; the larger the step, the greater the discontinuity and the more difficulty in managing it. Figure 2-2 (a) and (b) shows a sequence of S curves, each representing the development of an incremental process or product design improvement, each separated by a discontinuity. For each curve, there are two major phases: first the steep slope of the curve during the process of product development or process improvement, and then the leveling out as the new process approaches the limits of its capability. At that point, further improvements are difficult or impossible to achieve without developing a new process to take its place.

In every dynamic industry, these advances are occurring continually. The problem that is seriously handicapping U.S. companies today is that they are ill equipped to handle these advances. Our organizational structures, management processes, measurement and reward systems, and even our educational system are geared to a past era. Personnel policies and organizational structures erect barriers to learning. Independent compartments of the corporation inhibit dialogue and information transfer. We reward employees for individual success, not group accomplishment. We treat science, product design, and the production process as though they were separate, almost unrelated subjects. And management treats the technical parts of the product cycle as a matter of concern only to the technically trained specialist. These methods worked when technological progress was slow and when we had little international competition. They are still effective today in

Figure 2-2. Discontinuity and technical change.

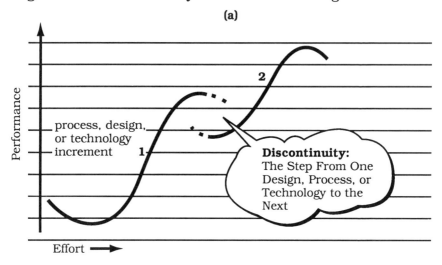

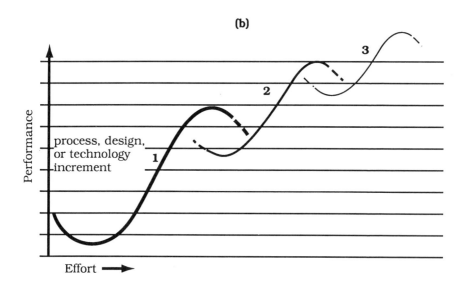

mature industries that have reached the peak of their technological S curves.

But these old methods will not work in the environment of increasing product complexity, intensive competition, and rapid, continual change. The product cycle, from the concept phase to production, involves the integration of all the groups involved in the marketing, development, and manufacturing process. It requires the direct participation of top management to make the total integrated system work. It demands new methods of measuring and rewarding performance.

New methods must be found to keep pace with the constant advances in product performance and changes in customer needs. Before a company's new product reaches a stable and tranquil period of maturity, its competitors will be preparing a new process, technology, or product advance to render that product obsolete. In order to lead or at least keep pace with this continual sequence of technical advancement, companies must learn how to cope with complexity and dynamic technological change. They must learn to manage the steep and slippery slope of the S curve.

The dramatic pace of this moving technology target is having a profound influence on how companies must manage the product cycle. It is the force that is driving corporate integration. It influences management behavior and responsibilities, organizational structures, skills, and personnel practices. Chapter 3 provides an overview of the entire cycle to place these principal issues in perspective.

Chapter 3

The Product Cycle: Critical Gears That Drive It

At the heart of the industrial corporation is the product cycle. It encompasses the entire range of a company's activities, including marketing, research, product development, quality assurance, manufacturing, and hundreds or thousands of suppliers. It comprises all the strategies, investments, decisions, and tasks necessary to create a new product. For all practical purposes, the product cycle *is* the company, since it contains the bulk of its resources. It is the engine that drives the corporation, generates revenue, determines profit, and supplies customers with what they want. Moving a new product through the cycle from initial concept through the complex corporate bureaucracy and out the door to the marketplace is an immensely complicated task. And U.S. industry simply takes too long to do it.

Two factors are key to understanding the product cycle: (1) the management and organizational *process* a company uses to allocate resources, assign tasks, monitor status, and make decisions; and (2) the *content* of the actual work that must be performed to plan strategies, develop technologies, design products, and measure results. Although both aspects are important to the success of a development program, no new product can succeed with weak work content. Strong skills in and emphasis on market strategy, applied research, product design, and manufacturing process are all of overarching importance to the success of a new product. These elements of a total management system, with the right intensity, the highest technical and management capability, the appropriate timing, and the necessary organizational methods, are all vital factors in determining the length of the product cycle and the cost and quality of the final product. In addition, the way all these elements are integrated into a unified management system is vital to the success of a new product program. For these reasons, most of the emphasis in this book is on these pivotal areas of content and how they relate to one another. But this chapter discusses the product cycle management process not only because it is important but because it provides a framework for showing how the principal areas of content fit into the overall company structure.

The Product Development Process

In order to visualize the product development process, the obvious first step is to study the corporate organizational chart. That document lists the company hierarchy, including all the departments, the department heads, where they report, and some identification of the function of each. Unfortunately, this document can be very deceptive. In principle, the organizational structure should facilitate the work of developing, manufacturing, and selling the product, and the chart should indicate who performs each part of that work. In practice, the chart does not always accomplish that function because it often does not define a product's actual path as it travels from its conception to delivery to the customer.

Because there is no visible road map to describe the route a product must take through the organizational hierarchy, it is not at all unusual for top executives to witness the passage of a new product from the laboratory through the factory and to the customer without really understanding how it got there and why it arrived so late. In addition, there is no simple method for monitoring, measuring, controlling, and executing the process of managing the cycle. Instead of using an overall strategy for the development of a product, management must rely on short-term tactics and reactive solutions in a crisis to nudge a program along. The result of this lack of structure can be a series of unrelated events, each leading to poor decisions, inadequate emphasis on the right tasks, and too much stress on the less important ones. In fact, the normal functional organizational structure presents many roadblocks to effective product development, and companies must look for ways to circumvent them.

In some companies, informal groups and alliances are formed for the purpose of overcoming barriers set up by the formal organization. Often the real centers of influence, channels of communication, and power to get things accomplished reside with people who are not even in the management hierarchy. Sometimes these operations are recognized and given some legitimacy by top management when it realizes that this is the only way the product can be developed. But informal relationships are usually too loose and temporary to be effective. Consequently, many companies are formalizing this type of ad hoc organization; they institute management processes that actually override the functional hierarchy. Known by such labels as product development process, these processes provide a formal mechanism for allocating resources and tasks, evaluating progress, and making program decisions.

To review all the details of such a product development process would require an astronomical volume of information. My intent is not to provide such a description. Even if all the details could be crammed between the covers of a single book, such an exhaustive treatment would be of little value. The answer to the problem of long cycles will not be found by reading such a mass of detail. To solve any problem, we need to get at its basic origin. In order to show the fundamental reasons and permanent solutions for long development cycles, this book will concentrate on those major elements of the cycle that are the most important and have the greatest leverage for shortening it. In order to gain some perspective on where and how these elements fit into the total range of activities that make up a corporate program to develop and manufacture products, it is helpful to look at the structure of a typical product development cycle and the management process to carry it out.

The Structure of the Product Cycle

To discuss its most important elements and how they relate to one another, we need to look at a series of "maps" of the total product cycle. These maps define its overall structure as well as the pivotal parts that make it work. They also describe the path each individual product must traverse from its conception to delivery to the marketplace. The product cycle is quite different for each company, since its detail is determined by the technology, product line, chain of command, organization, size, degree of geographical dispersal, and management style. Therefore, the description given here is not intended to be definitive. Rather it serves as a framework around which to organize the discussion of the critical elements of the cycle.

Figure 3-1 shows a diagram of the overall structure of the product cycle with headings of its three major components. The unlabeled rectangles depict the plans, strategies, tasks, resources, and decisions necessary to translate a new product concept into a marketable entity. All these events and activities are grouped into three categories or levels as indicated on the chart:

Level A: Product life cycle decisions
Level B: Technology development process
Level C: Product development process

Each of these three categories is critical to the conduct of any product program. But despite the fact that they are listed as separate entities and depicted as sequential, in reality, they are highly interactive and interdependent, and the lines of demarcation between them must be practically nonexistent. These invisible boundaries are the key to corporate integration.

In order to understand the composition of each level, the interactions between them, and their importance to the entire product development process, it is necessary to look at each in more detail, including how each applies to the development of a product.

Figure 3-1. Product life cycle.

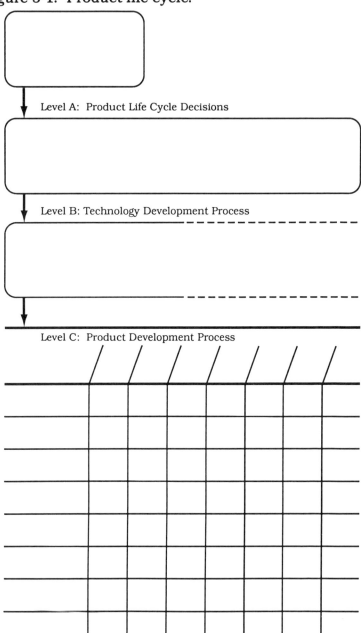

Level A: Product Life Cycle Decisions

Level B: Technology Development Process

Level C: Product Development Process

Level A: The Product Life Cycle Decisions

Figure 3-2 shows the elements of Level A, the product life cycle decisions, in greater detail. The blocks define the specific steps higher management must take in directing the overall product program. Managing the cycle from beginning to end entails a series of difficult decisions that involve risks and determine the future course of the program as well as the company's future revenue and profitability. The decisions about what risks to take, what investments to make, when to proceed to the next step in the cycle, and if and when to terminate a program must be made with a combination of information and management judgment. The strategies, plans, and decisions identified in Level A are vital elements in the product development cycle. Not only do they require an extraordinary amount of supporting data, they also demand intensive top executive involvement in a program.

The Level A strategies and decisions on funding, timing of program initiation, design approval, major capital investments, commitments on product performance, and timing of production and customer delivery are critical to the pace and final success of a program. Missteps in any one of these areas can have an adverse, even disastrous, impact on a new product program. Yet the soundness of these decisions is almost totally dependent on the accuracy of the data and on the objectivity, judgment, and expertise of the participants in the activities of Levels A and B. Consequently, the communications and dialogue that must occur between Levels A, B, and C become a critical part of the project management process. The traditional remoteness of top management from the engineering and manufacturing groups implementing its decisions is no longer workable. The executives in Level A and the sales, technical, and manufacturing people on the firing line are all major players contributing to a project's success.

Level B: The Technology Development Process

The activities in Level B of the process (Figure 3-3), usually carried out in an applied research laboratory or an ad-

(text continues on page 30)

Figure 3-2. Level A: product life cycle decisions.

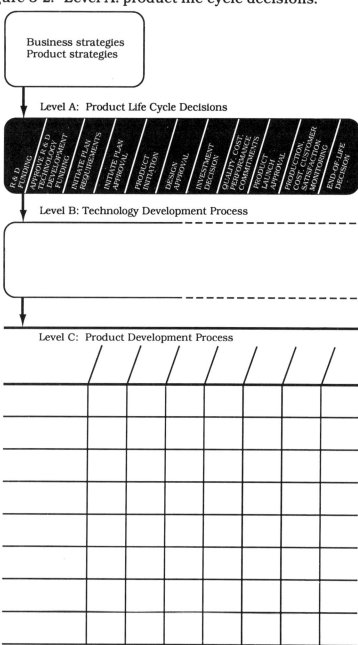

Figure 3-3. Level B: technology development process.

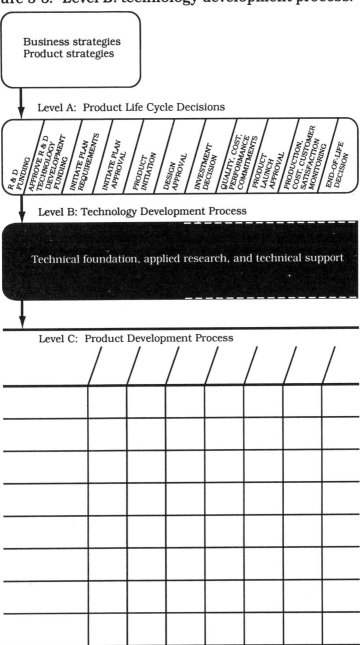

vanced development department, provide the technical knowledge and foundation that support a new product program. They can also furnish the continuing technical support that is an essential ingredient to successful product and process design and manufacturing. The degree of investment in this level will, of course, depend on the nature of the product and the degree of technological advancement. In all but minor increments in product advances, this technical knowledge is critical to the future success of the product cycle. The investment in this work is relatively small compared to the investment in the remainder of the product cycle, but its importance and leverage are enormous.

And despite the past physical and organizational isolation of the research laboratory from the rest of the corporation, the activities in Level B must become directly and tightly bonded to the activities of the other two levels. The Level A decision makers must rely on the research efforts of those functioning at Level B—their knowledge and insights—to assess the scientific basis, technical status, risks, and technical feasibility of new products and technologies. Level B must also provide the technical foundation and support to the Level C groups that will design and produce the products. Level B is essentially the technical bridge between top management and the design, development, and manufacturing activities in Level C. Consequently, top management and the research laboratories are not ancillary and remote activities. They must be direct participants.

Level C: The Product Development Process

The bulk of the technical and manufacturing personnel and capital resources expenditures required to launch a product, as well as the actual implementation of the details of the development program, take place in Level C. This level (Figure 3-4) contains the core of the development program—the design and manufacturing engineering teams that translate the strategies, market requirements, technical knowledge, and product concept into a manufacturable and marketable product. Level C consists of a series of program phases, ap-

Figure 3-4. Level C: product development process.

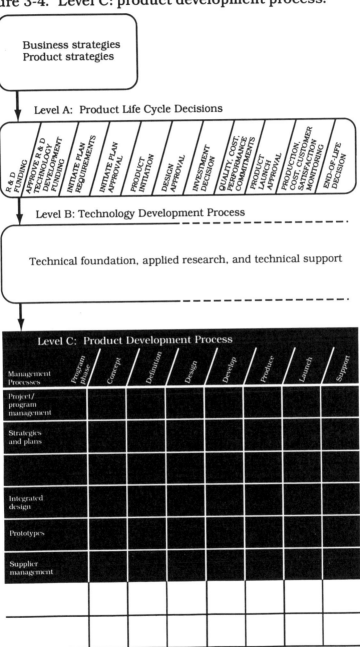

pearing horizontally across the top of the chart, including the product concept, definition, design, development, production, product launch to the customer, and support of the product in the marketplace. Each of these phases progresses sequentially with time as the program proceeds. Checkpoints are set at the completion of each phase. At each point management evaluates the status of the program and decides whether that phase has been satisfactorily completed before proceeding to the next.

A list of management "processes" is shown vertically at the left side of the chart. Appropriate activities for each process would be listed in the blocks under the appropriate program phases. A true process chart including all the activities under each phase would be much more complicated—illustrating a management challenge of immense proportions. The mechanics and process of planning, administering, and executing these details are awesome. It is for this reason alone that some form of disciplined management process is needed (in all but the smallest companies making the simplest types of products) to control and carry out these activities. By dividing the program into measurable stages and checkpoints, management can more effectively monitor progress and make decisions on how and when to proceed to the next phase.

The Role of the Program Manager

This type of formal, documented management process is valuable, but it is far from sufficient. Its complexity demands a focused and powerful leadership. Since the groups participating in the total process exist at many levels of the management hierarchy, are spread widely throughout the corporation, owe their allegiances to many different constituencies, and are often organizationally and geographically dispersed, only the strongest leader can make it work. The responsibilities of formulating strategy, expediting decisions, coordinating, planning, scheduling, assessing status, measuring progress, and taking corrective action are enormous. The most common method of coping with this awesome management job is to appoint a project or program manager to orchestrate and administer the entire product development process. This responsibility spans almost the entire spectrum of the corporation, including marketing, development, manufacturing, and even suppliers.

But making that responsibility even more challenging is the fact that the process is different for every product. The product development process I have outlined needs to be customized and adapted. Differences in the nature of a product's performance objectives, technology content, degree of technical advance, market, method of purchase, and many other factors will determine how the program should be managed. For example, a new product with major technological advances requires a strong research involvement, but one incorporating only minor incremental change may need no research support at all. The process of developing a product whose parts are purchased externally differs considerably from a program that develops the entire product in-house. Recognizing these differences and making the necessary adaptations are the responsibility of the program manager. His or her success can have a major influence on the length of the cycle and quality of the product.

Despite the fact that there are many well-developed tools available to assist in carrying out this complex job, it is a very difficult one. Although these managers assume a heavy responsibility for the success of their respective products, few if any of the line operations report directly to them. Consequently, their position does not automatically endow them with the authority to allocate resources, make decisions, and directly manage the individual groups involved in carrying out the work. Instead, they must derive their power from three sources: (1) top management, which must give them strong support and a great deal of authority; (2) their own stature in the company, which must be high enough to give them personal power over the groups involved in the product cycle; and (3) strong, stable, and permanent teams of the most committed and capable people from the key functions involved in the program. These three assets are mandatory if the project manager is to be successful.

How Well Does the Product Development Process Work?

Although it is too early to accurately measure the results, an increasing number of companies are instituting some version of this type of formal management process. Such a formal management control system, if properly used, can be very helpful, and, in some companies, it is essential. The product cycle is simply too complex to execute in an unstructured, uncontrolled environment of laissez-faire. This process can give discipline to the management function. It forces the management team to carefully think through each step and ensure that there is enough substantive data and proof of the true status of the program before making the next decision.

However, there are some potential pitfalls in the use of such an "extra-organizational" management structure. Although this type of formal process is intended to shorten the product cycle, it can actually have the opposite effect. In some companies, the passage from one phase of the cycle to the next requires a long list of signatures on an approval document. Sometimes these signatories choose to play it safe and err on the side of caution, and each checkpoint in the process becomes an impassable barrier—a safe procedural haven from decision making. Constant delays and endless debates, compounded by a long list of required approvals, can slow down a program. This type of rigidity can stifle creativity and flexibility, preventing management from taking risks and being innovative. On the other hand, other companies set up a structured process and then take excessive risks by bypassing the controls and checkpoints in the system in an attempt to expedite the program. Either extreme has its hazards, and it takes a strong company management to overcome them.

A structured management process by itself, even if it is well managed, will not bring about shorter development cycles. It is only a road map—telling you where you must go next and whether you are ready for the next stage of the trip. The key to a successful product cycle is the content and application of selected, strategic factors of the total process. These elements form the critical path to shorter development cycles, and they will be the focus of this book.

The Critical Elements of the Product Cycle

Designing and manufacturing a product is similar to erecting a building. The building's construction entails the following steps, in order:

1. An architectural design
2. A foundation
3. A building skeleton, with steel beams, girders, and columns
4. The outside masonry walls
5. Interior finishing, decorating, and furnishing

Each step in the sequence is totally dependent on the satisfactory completion of the previous steps. It would be unthinkable to erect the skeleton without the foundation, or the walls without the steel beams and columns.

The design, development, and manufacture of products using today's advanced technologies require the same systematic approach: a strong technical foundation, a design of the highest quality, and a systematic series of steps from the concept of the product to its delivery to the customer. Any attempts to deemphasize or bypass any of the critical steps of the product cycle will create enormous problems when the product reaches the manufacturing floor and the customer's office or home.

In the building of a skyscraper or the manufacture of an automobile, a computer, an airplane, or almost any other product, the most important part of the product cycle is the beginning, not the end. That is when the foundation is laid for every other step to the marketplace. The strength of that foundation will determine success or failure.

Out of the long catalogue of individual jobs and responsibilities required to successfully carry out a product cycle, there is one critical path of key, high-leverage areas that are essential to the success of a new product program and are the major factors in reducing the development cycle. These critical areas of the business must be the healthiest. Otherwise, nothing a company does to prop up a weak or failing program will work.

Figure 3-5 shows the same map of the product development process, identifying these six key areas:

1. *Technical foundation: applied research.* The technical foundation for the product cycle; the development of basic scientific and technical knowledge required to design manufacturable, high-quality products in the shortest period of time; the prerequisite technical basis for every other step; a close and continuous partner with all other participants throughout the entire cycle.

2. *The strategic direction: management of change and risk.* The matching of the product direction and the customer needs; the choice of the degree of product and technology advance required to develop new generations of models through manageable, methodical, technically feasible increments, each built on the foundation laid by the preceding one. These decisions can have a profound influence on cycle length.

3. *Integrated product and process design.* For performance, manufacturability, and quality—building into the product design a manufacturing process that will reproduce that design under high production conditions at low cost and high quality.

4. *Prototypes.* Analysis of physical models of the total, integrated product to evaluate design, process, and component interactions that are complex, unpredictable, and difficult to simulate by other means.

5. *Key investment decisions.* How and when to make major capital investments. There are hazards in making these decisions too early or too late.

6. *Integration of the supplier.* The supplier of critical components must become virtually a part of the company it serves.

We may well believe that these six factors are merely restatements of what we already know. There is nothing new about prototypes, product design, research, strategy, or closer supplier relations. And if we were to poll a cross section of company executives to determine whether they were investing in these activities, the answers would be overwhelmingly

Figure 3-5. Six key areas of the product development process.

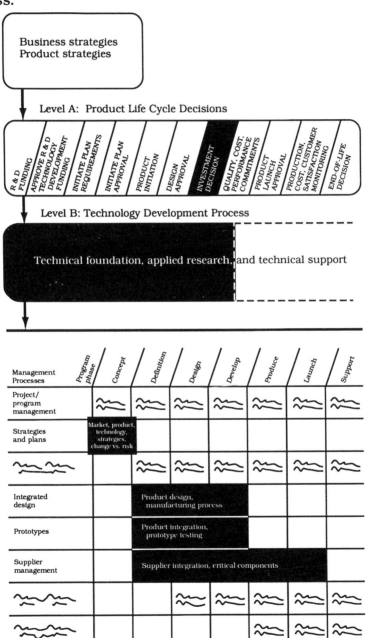

affirmative. But if we were to ask them how successful they have been in implementing them, and how effective they have been in achieving shorter developments cycles, the answers would be much less positive.

Companies are having difficulty implementing these six concepts because the activities involved have acquired new dimensions that make their application much more complicated. Advancing technology, complexity, and product performance are changing the meaning of these activities. In order to carry them out successfully, we need to understand their new dimensions and more subtle aspects.

Finally, merely budgeting for these activities and assigning people to perform them is not enough. Another ingredient in the successful application of these factors is the emphasis management gives to them. The ultimate measure of this emphasis is the priority given to these parts of the development cycle, the magnitude of the resources allocated to them, the intensity of the activity in each of them, and the manner in which management orchestrates and integrates them.

In the following chapters, I explore each of these six elements of the critical path.

Chapter 4

Strategic Direction: Management of Change and Risk

An ancient Chinese proverb states that a journey of a thousand miles begins with a single step. At the time of origin of this prescient observation, it is highly unlikely that such a concept as a product cycle existed. Nevertheless, the product cycle, like the proverbial thousand-mile journey, is long and arduous, and the first step may well be the most important. Like a racehorse that stumbles at the starting gate, a company that falters at the beginning of the product cycle may never regain the stride and pace to enable it to catch up with its competitors. In a hotly competitive industry, a false move at the beginning may preordain extensive delays later, and even loss of market share. Creation of the market, product, and technology strategies is the first critical element in the process.

The process of defining the strategic marketing and product goals is important because it determines the direction and sets in motion all subsequent parts of the product cycle. If the strategy is poorly conceived or if the company vacillates too long in selecting the direction it wants to take, the product cycle can become an uncontrolled series of mishaps and miscalculations.

The Key Strategic Issues

At the beginning of any new product program, management must address three issues, each of which has a major influence on the length of the product cycle:

1. How to make the product concept and performance specifications responsive to the market and customer needs
2. How to know when and how to decide among several possible design alternatives
3. How to determine the magnitude of the technical and performance advances that can be achieved with acceptable risk (Figure 4-1)

Matching Product Concept and Performance Specifications to Market Needs

The major purpose of any business is to market products its customers want. Yet one of the most widespread problems cited by management in widely different industries is the difficulty in identifying and specifying such products. The reason lies in the traditional functional organization with its lack of interaction and dialogue between marketing, engineering, and manufacturing. Because of this separation, product programs are pushed forward aggressively, while market and business strategies are developed independently. The result of these divergent paths is that the product concepts and designs have little relationship to the needs of the marketplace. A product may reach an advanced stage of development before the company discovers that there is no demand for it, or that the competition has scooped it with a better one. The only way a company can recoup from such a blunder is to redesign the product to more closely match customer needs and try to rush through the product cycle again. But the schedule will be delayed, and the consequences of attempting to expedite the program too hastily can be disastrous.

Although this mismatch between the marketing strategy and the other key parts of the product cycle is a major problem, this chasm is narrowing in some corporations. Many of

Figure 4-1. Strategic direction.

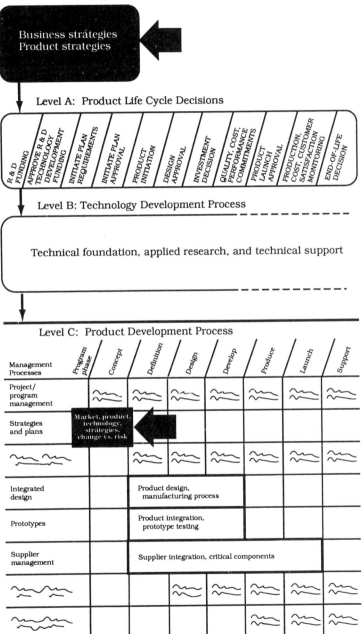

the companies reviewed in Appendix B are putting more emphasis on the development of marketing and product strategies. They believe that this increased concentration on strategy early in the product program is an important step toward shortening their product cycles. Some are decentralizing their organizations by creating business units, with each unit dedicated to a different product and each containing the marketing, engineering, and manufacturing operations. Others are making marketing an equal partner with engineering and manufacturing in cross-functional teams. In the Gemini Consulting surveys (see Appendix A), one of the two most frequently listed steps selected by companies to strengthen and shorten their product cycles was an increased emphasis on marketing and product strategies.

Deciding Which Product Alternative to Pursue

At the beginning of a new program, many companies, particularly those with an abundance of good ideas and plenty of capital and technical skills, launch competing product designs. Some actually form two or more teams, each pursuing its respective approach. Management cheers them on, expecting that the competitive spirit will create the impetus needed to develop a superior product. It is also hoped that this plan will result in a greater chance of success, because at least one of the designs should be a winner, even if the others fail. The problem with this approach lies in the inability of management to make up its mind on which design to select. The competition among teams intensifies and can become not only technical but political. Because of management's indecision, precious technical and production resources are spread thin across the competing programs; the necessary intensive design, development, and preparation for manufacturing cannot be carried out. When the final decision is made, too much of the scheduled time to implement the product cycle has already been wasted, and the timetable for customer delivery has slipped badly. In addition, the losing sides often continue to fight to keep their alternative approaches alive, frittering away more valuable resources.

From the late 1960s through the 1970s, IBM frequently maintained alternative approaches to product designs. For example, the company pursued the development of three alternative means of achieving greater computer memory capacity and performance, including ferrite cores, field effect transistors (FETs), and bipolar arrays. All three approaches competed for use in future computer systems until the latter was finally selected. Companies that can afford to carry on this parallel strategy can profit by it only if management knows when to make an irrevocable decision. That decision must be made early in the program using the most informed marketing, research, engineering, and manufacturing advice. When it is made, the entire corporation must join in aggressively pursuing the long and difficult steps toward customer delivery. But if management vacillates and equivocates, the product cycle will be lengthened.

Determining the Magnitude of Technical and Performance Advances With Manageable Risk

How large a technical step should be taken in a new product? The answer to this question is not obvious, and there is no easy formula to use. Yet it can have a major impact on the length of the product cycle, and it is *the* factor that can make or break a program. A wrong decision can destine a project to failure, no matter how much money and resources are expended to save it.

The size of the technical step to be taken from one product to the next will determine the direction, cost, and risk of any new product venture. The decisions about what new features to incorporate, what new processes to use, and what advances in performance to achieve involve some of the most serious hazards to the success of the product cycle. If a company sets goals that are too ambitious, the program may be doomed to constant delays and cost overruns. On the other hand, if management plays it too safe by instituting only marginally incremental changes, the company will greatly increase its ability to meet production schedules—but lose the market to more aggressive competitors.

Chapter 2 discussed the problem of overcoming discontinuities between old and new process and technology advances. Some companies attempt to leap too quickly over too large a discontinuity, often with a weak technical base or inadequate skills to support such a leap. Each significant change in product design or production process involves some level of discontinuity and requires a new period of learning. The larger the discontinuity, the greater the learning required to cross over it—and the greater the risk of failure.

The manner in which companies manage risk and product advances by mastering these discontinuities is critical to the conduct of the product cycle. Practically every product introduction requires some new advanced design concept, more components, an additional subsystem, a new manufacturing process, or a change in materials. The degree of technological advance that each change represents and the number of changes that are introduced simultaneously determine the degree of risk in launching a new product.

There is a continuing debate concerning the most effective means of advancing technology and maintaining leadership in the race for competitiveness. On the one hand are the proponents of a great leap forward, a major advance in technology. They believe that by taking such a giant and precipitous step all at once, a company can outpace its competition and seize industry leadership. On the other hand is the group that believes that success can best be achieved by an incremental strategy in which smaller, measured advances are made, each based on the foundation laid by the previous one.

The first approach is equivalent to a technological revolution. It is more dramatic, but it is very risky and, depending on the magnitude of the proposed advance, it seldom works. The second method is methodical, logical, and undramatic. It is far more predictable and, best of all, it succeeds. Professor Robert Hayes of the Harvard Business School compares the two approaches to the tortoise and the hare. "U.S. companies do, however, tend to adopt approaches toward the strategic leap end; those of our two most powerful international competitors, Germany and Japan, tend to seek incremental improvements within an existing structure and technology. They are the tortoise; we are the hare. In the fable, as we may recall with some apprehension, the tortoise won the race. Are we to share the hare's fate?"[1]

Chapter 2 cited the internal combustion engine and the silicon chip as examples of the history of the incremental character of technology and product advancement. Despite the revolutionary nature of these technology breakthroughs, each step in their advancement was carefully and methodically built on the foundation laid by the previous advance. Any company that attempted to bypass these incremental steps risked failure. A recent example of incremental, tortoiselike advance is Honda's achievement of a fifty-five-miles-per-gallon "lean burn" engine. U.S. automakers believed that this type of performance required a major breakthrough, but Honda accomplished it with incremental modifications to existing technology.

Figure 4-2 illustrates different levels of risks. These levels range from low-risk evolutionary change to very high-risk revolutionary advance. Very few companies attempt revolution in one product generation, and when they do, as will be shown in some later examples, they almost always fail. Companies in competitive industries will most likely not advance their products through very slow evolutionary means either. Those that do will almost always lose the market to their fleeter competitors. What must be considered is the effect of varying degrees of incremental change on the length of the product cycle and the ultimate marketability and quality of the product. Company management faces major challenges in assessing the magnitude and number of these incremental advances and the risk they entail.

New Product Change: How It Influences the Product Cycle

The decision on the degree of change in a new product is the first of the critical elements of the product development cycle. How this element influences the length of the cycle can be

---

1. Robert H. Hayes, "Strategic Planning—Forward in Reverse?" *Harvard Business Review,* November/December 1985, p. 116.

Figure 4-2. Levels of discontinuity and risk (one product generation).

Evolutionary

1. *Evolutionary—Low Risk*

   - Small dimensional changes
   - Addition of a few standard components
   - Minor changes in etching, cleaning, heat-treating processes

---

Incremental

2. *Incremental— Moderate Risk*

   - Introduction of one or two significant new inventions, important process changes, design features
   - Addition of major new subsystem
   - Significant increase in density of parts, size reduction

3. *Incremental—High Risk*

   - Introduction of four or five significant new inventions, major process changes, or design features
   - Addition of two or three major new subsystems
   - Major changes in materials of several key components

Revolutionary

4. *Revolutionary—Very High Risk*

   - Major change in principles of operation
   - Major change in technology

illustrated by noting how too many aggressive and high-risk changes affect other parts of the cycle. The chapters indicated discuss each of these factors in detail.

1. *The technical foundation (Chapter 5).* If the change is too drastic, the research and development resources will not be sufficient to build a strong enough technical base for a successful program. The adverse effects of that weak foundation will permeate throughout the product cycle, making each of the subsequent steps of product design, product integration and prototyping, and pilot production increasingly difficult to complete successfully.

2. *Integrated product design (Chapter 6).* If the technical foundation is too weak, even the best team of design and manufacturing engineers will be unable to achieve a good design that will be manufacturable and reliable. Processes will be impossible to control, yields will be low, uniformity of product characteristics will be poor, and trade-offs between the process and the design will be difficult to achieve.

3. *Product integration and prototyping (Chapter 7).* If the technical foundation is weak and the product design poor, successful integration of the product will be all but impossible to achieve. Attempts to simulate performance, build and test prototypes, analyze and diagnose defects, and operate these models to the product specifications will result in lengthy experimentation and an extended period of redesign.

The upshot of all these problems will be a voluminous and continuing flow of engineering changes, constant program slippages, and intolerable program costs. All these severe barriers to the progress of the product cycle will greatly hamper, and possibly prevent, company management from investing in the manufacturing equipment needed to scale up production (Chapter 9). The end result could even be failure and the end of the program.

In many instances, the consequences of being overaggressive are less dramatic. The problems may go undiscovered until well into the product cycle. In fact, certain types of defects or design flaws may not be recognized until sufficient numbers of prototype or pilot models are produced and enough statistical evidence is obtained. There will be no warning alarm that suddenly goes off, signaling serious trouble; there will be no instant failure. The more likely result is that the consequences of excessive aggressiveness will slowly eat away at the program, creating an inexorable escalation of problems in yield, cost, quality, and schedule.

Bypassing the Increments: Why It Is Risky

If you have ever hiked up a high mountain, you know how easy it is to be deceived by the initial ease of the ascent: The trail is smooth and wide, the weather sunny and warm, and the incline surprisingly gradual. But a few hours later, the trail disappears and the terrain becomes rocky, slippery, and steep. The temperature plummets to freezing levels, and thunderclaps and lightning begin to threaten. An inexperienced hiker who is poorly equipped for such a risky venture can suffer serious consequences in the face of these conditions.

Starting a risky new product is analogous to the mountain climb of an inexperienced hiker. The beginning of the program appears to be tantalizingly simple. Innovative and well-trained engineers and technicians in the laboratory—after lengthy experimentation, careful choice of materials, meticulous crafting of parts, and expert assembly of a model—prove that the product will work. This, by itself, is a major accomplishment. But its success can be deceptive. As the project proceeds into the subsequent phases of design, process development, prototype testing, and pilot production, the consequences of biting off more than you can chew begin to appear. For example:

- Fine dimensions, well controlled in the pristine and expert environment of the research laboratory, cannot be reproduced in higher volume assembly with less skilled labor and the less controlled conditions of a pilot line or factory.
- Previously undetected failure modes or yield problems begin to appear as additional tests are conducted under

conditions of greater stress than those occurring in the laboratory.

- Small samples of very pure materials, which were carefully selected so that they worked in the laboratory, become difficult to reproduce in large quantities because of the variability of the characteristics in high production.
- The "window" within which the product was designed is too narrow to permit quantities of the product to be produced, since the variability of the components' characteristics is too great to ensure a reasonable yield.
- When too many new and untried components and subsystems are attempted at once, the probability of problems when the total product is assembled is greatly increased. Even though the product works in the laboratory under the watchful eyes of skilled personnel, many random defects begin to occur throughout the design cycle.
- There are far too few skilled management, engineering, and trained technical and factory employees to cope with the large number of major advances that are attempted simultaneously.

Like an inexperienced mountain climber, companies encountering these types of problems misjudged the magnitude of the task and were unprepared to cope with the difficulty and complexity ahead. They made a strategic decision to commit to major product advances that were based on too little data, a poor technical foundation, and an inadequate organization.

Some companies opt for radical changes in technology far too quickly, hoping to score a grand slam over their competitors, and usually with the misguided belief that they may actually succeed. A notable example was the attempt by Trilogy Ltd. in the early 1980s to bypass interim steps in silicon integrated circuit and computer technology by building an entire computer on a single wafer of silicon. The program failed, not only because the company did not have the technical capability to make it work, but because the worldwide silicon industry did not have the technical knowledge or experience to make such a bold step a reality. Despite the dramatic advances of the preceding twenty years, the control of materials and processes used in constructing integrated circuits was still not sufficient to achieve the yields needed to make this product. Even Trilogy's founder, Gene Amdahl, admitted that it had attempted too many technological changes too fast.[2] Some day in the future, the technical foundation in silicon materials and processes may become sufficiently strong for the Trilogy concept to work. But it is more likely to succeed only after several incremental advances in semiconductor integrated circuit technology are successfully achieved.

General Motors' unsuccessful attempt in the 1980s to completely automate some assembly lines was another example of an attempt to achieve low costs and market advantage with a precipitous advance in technology.[3] Many companies try less dramatic advances in their products but still experience some degree of failure, although it may be less visible and more difficult to evaluate. A risky program may achieve some success in the marketplace, but with considerable penalties, such as longer product cycles, higher costs, lower profit margins, or loss of market share even though the product may not completely fail.

How much change is too much? What level of product complexity is unmanageable? There is no simple measurement. Such an evaluation involves a complex assessment of many quantitative and judgmental factors. Even with the most expert advice and the most complete set of data, the conclusions will not always be precise. Furthermore, competitors may play a part in the decision; they may set such a fast pace of technology and product advancement that the only option is to take risks to keep up with them.

Many of the companies interviewed for this book, including DuPont, Eastman Kodak, and Caterpillar, have learned from experience and are taking a more cautious approach to technological change. As one of their strategies to shorten the development cycle and increase success, they are reducing the

2. Rosalind Klein Berlin, "Gene Amdahl Fights," *Fortune,* 1 September 1986.
3. Mary Ann Keller, *Rude Awakening* (New York: William Morrow and Co., 1989).

number of inventions and major technology and process improvements in one product. There is no magic formula that can be used as a guideline, but some of these companies are limiting their new products to three inventions and no more than 20 percent new components.

Of course, establishing a level of acceptable risk requires much more than such simple arithmetic. Only one major breakthrough invention or only a 10 percent change in components could result in a high level of risk, or four or five relatively small incremental innovations and a large number of minor parts replacements could be quite manageable. Each change must be assessed on its own merits.

A Method for Evaluating Change and Its Risks

Despite the difficulty in making an accurate judgment about how much change is too much, new product risk can be reduced by careful evaluation of a few key factors. The following guidelines are meant to illustrate the type of information that will help you assess that risk. Although they are applicable to a wide range of industries, they can be revised as needed to fit a particular field. A level of change that is too risky for one type of product may be acceptable for another. A substantial advance could be devastating to a company weak in experience and technical skills, but much less risky for a company with a strong management and technical team and a good track record of success. Consequently, this evaluation method does not provide a precise gauge like a scale or a thermometer. Rather it presents a few guidelines that can be studied and used in consultation with experts. This method will help you assess:

- The most critical changes and advances that create the greatest opportunities to compete but also the greatest risk to a product's success
- The parts of the product design and manufacturing processes requiring the greatest emphasis and the most resources

- The degree of risk accompanying the present plans
- What must be done to reduce that risk

Identifying the Critical Changes

First, list the most critical changes from current product models that you plan to introduce in the next new product. Critical changes are those that:

- Constitute significant advances from previous products.
- Represent the most advanced state of the art.
- Present the greatest technical challenge.
- Are most important to the product's performance.
- Need the most intensive development effort.

These changes could fall under the following categories:

- Design features
- Dimensions and tolerances
- Production processes
- Materials
- Components
- Subsystems
- Software

Evaluating the Level of Risk

Next, for each of the critical changes, rate the level of risk involved on a scale from 0 to 10 (with 0 being the least risky, 10 the most risky). In order to assign such a rating, consider several factors that can influence the degree of risk:

- *The technical and scientific basis and support for the change.*
—A change that appears relatively minor could actually entail a sizable risk if there is little technical understanding of or experience with it; for example, the use of a polymer that is purchased "off the shelf" from a supplier simply because it seems to work in the laboratory could seriously affect yield or reliability.

—Conversely, a more profound change could actually be less risky if there is a strong technical basis for it.

• *The degree of previous experience with the change, both within the company and in other companies.* If the change is sizable but it has previously been incorporated in other products successfully, the risk of using it in a new product is reduced. Even if you have no experience with it, your risk is reduced to some extent if other companies have such experience. Knowing that it can be done successfully is an important factor in establishing the credibility of such an advance, even though you will still need to develop it for your own products.

• *Proximity of the performance and physical specifications to the limits of the technology.* The closer a design approaches the limits of technology, the greater the risk. A design may have limits in temperature of operation, physical stress, tolerance for electrical breakdown, metal fatigue, and so on. If product strategy requires that the product be designed too close to these limits, the risk will be high.

Figure 4-3 illustrates three alternative results of such an

Figure 4-3. Risk evaluation.

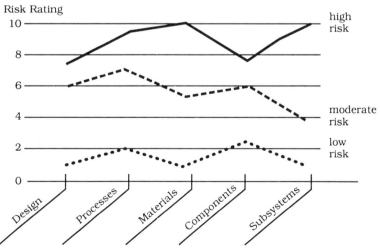

New Product Features

evaluation ranging from high to low risk. What is important about this type of assessment is not the numerical rating but the detailed analysis that must be carried out to develop the rating. No simple number can be the sole basis for a company's strategic decisions. Any final decisions on strategy must be based on data, judgment, experience, insight, market conditions, competition, and even a bit of intuition. Furthermore, the validity of the decision will be almost totally dependent on the experience and skills of the management making it. However, regardless of the method used, a careful evaluation of proposed product advances should be an essential ingredient in the development of strategy. The thoughtfulness with which you make these analyses will be a major factor in building the foundation for a shorter development cycle and a successful new product.

Chapter 5

Research: The Technical Foundation

Every structure needs a strong foundation, whether it is a bridge, a building, a computer, or an automobile. A skyscraper built on sand will look sparkling and new at the dedication ceremony, but cracks will soon cover the walls and plaster will begin to fall from the ceilings. The technical foundation that is needed to support the development and manufacturing of today's new products is equally important. It is an indispensable ingredient and a major building block of the product cycle (Figure 5-1). A new product can be rushed to market, bypassing the intensive work that is involved in building its foundation, and it will look fresh and stylish in the showroom, but serious defects will appear quickly, and the manufacturer will have some very unhappy customers. The entire process of planning, developing, manufacturing, and marketing a product is based on the foundation of technical knowledge that supports it. Without that foundation, no company can stay ahead of its best foreign and domestic competitors. Establishing the technical basis for a new product or technology is one of the most important steps on the critical path in the cycle that converts an invention to a manufacturable and marketable entity.

In the past, the need for this strong technical base was less urgent. Not only were manufactured products less complex, but major U.S. industries such as automobiles and electronics encountered far less foreign competition and thus could set the pace of progress and the standards of performance, cost, and quality. Furthermore, there was no Ralph

Figure 5-1. Foundation for competitiveness: applied research.

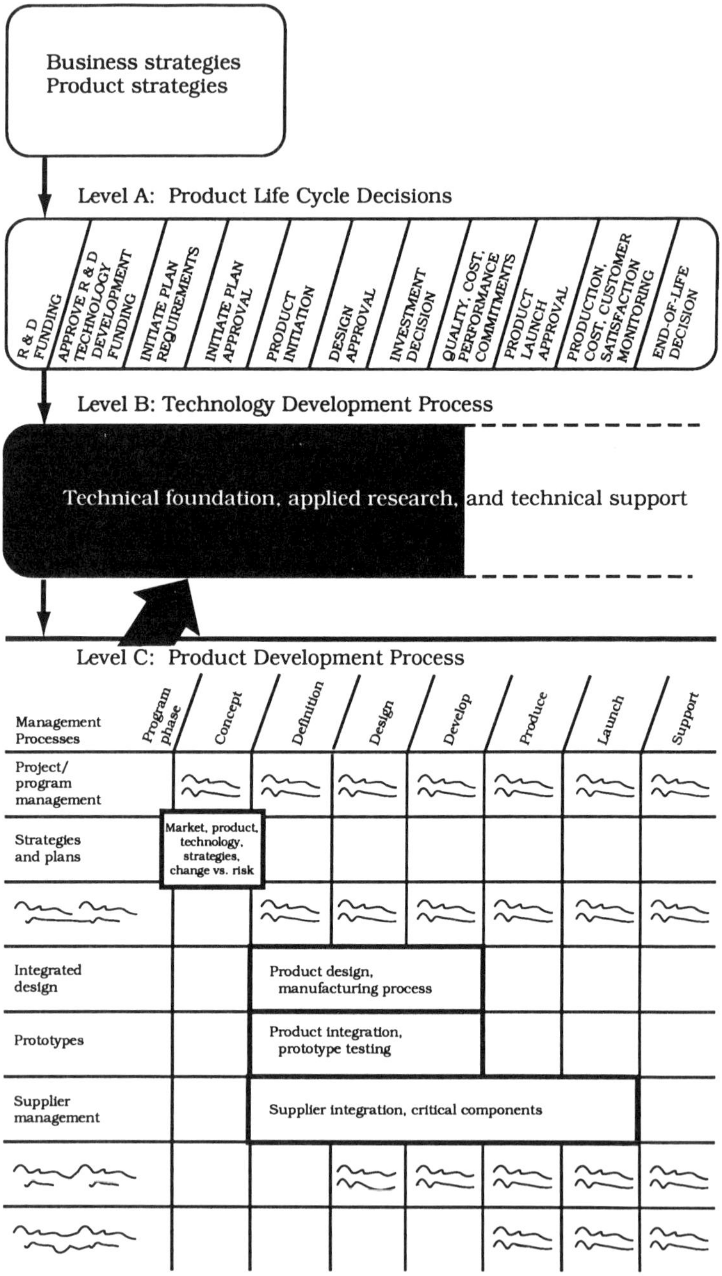

Business strategies
Product strategies

Level A:　Product Life Cycle Decisions

R & D FUNDING / APPROVE R & D TECHNOLOGY DEVELOPMENT FUNDING / INITIATE PLAN REQUIREMENTS / INITIATE PLAN APPROVAL / PRODUCT INITIATION / DESIGN APPROVAL / INVESTMENT DECISION / QUALITY, COST, PERFORMANCE COMMITMENTS / PRODUCT LAUNCH APPROVAL / PRODUCTION, COST, CUSTOMER SATISFACTION MONITORING / END-OF-LIFE DECISION

Level B: Technology Development Process

Technical foundation, applied research, and technical support

Level C:　Product Development Process

Management Processes	Program phase	Concept	Definition	Design	Develop	Produce	Launch	Support
Project/ program management								
Strategies and plans		Market, product, technology, strategies, change vs. risk						
Integrated design			Product design, manufacturing process					
Prototypes			Product integration, prototype testing					
Supplier management			Supplier integration, critical components					

Nader to challenge them, and the movement toward stiffer environmental laws and safety standards was just beginning.

The world has changed radically since then. Worldwide competition has greatly intensified, technology and product performance have skyrocketed, and consumer demands and expectations have increased enormously. The companies that can satisfy these new demands will be the winners. In this competitive environment, even a slight margin of superiority over competitors will be sufficient to increase market share. And this superiority can be achieved in part by building a stronger technical foundation for products than competitors.

Technical weakness is an almost certain guarantee of product development cycles that are long, costly, and often doomed to failure. In fact, many of the design and process problems that cripple a product program and create extensive delays can be traced to an inadequate technical understanding of the materials and processes used in the product design. Even the more conventional manufacturing issues of excessive work-in-process inventories, numerous engineering changes, production bottlenecks, high levels of rework, low yields, and poor equipment reliability can often be attributed to technical problems that were never fully understood or solved. Often such difficulties are not discovered until it is too late in the program to avoid delays. In many cases, the problems are so severe and require so much time to solve that they override in importance any other factors that may create schedule slippages and program delays. Since these problems often exist because of serious technical weaknesses, they cannot be eliminated by normal emergency methods such as cutting inventories, removing bottlenecks, expediting the delivery of parts, scheduling more overtime, buying extra equipment, or streamlining procedures. They often require the application of a great deal of technical expertise, study, and experimentation and a lengthy period of trial and error before a solution can be found.

Every company has had more than its fair share of unexpected and unwelcome technical surprises. Many of these result from the fact that there was simply not enough experience with or understanding of the technology or processes used in the product. They can also be caused by vendor communications problems. Although the following products were ultimately successful, they illustrate the types of problems that even the best of companies can encounter:

* ABBOTT LABORATORIES developed a product that measures blood chemistry parameters such as cholesterol and potassium and can actually be used in the doctor's office. This product takes a sample of blood, separates the blood into cells and plasma, measures a small quantity of plasma, and mixes it with a reagent inside a plastic cartridge. The resulting chemical change can be read optically in a matter of minutes, enabling the doctor to give the patient quick feedback and recommendations for remedial action, if necessary.

During the course of development of the potassium test, while testing the entire system, Abbott unexpectedly discovered a serious defect. Unknown to Abbott, in order to improve the mechanical characteristics of the cartridge, the supplier had changed the plasticizer. Unfortunately, the substitution of this new material led to problems in the chemistry of the reagent and the plasma, which resulted in inaccurate measurements, a totally unacceptable situation for this type of product.

* CORNING INCORPORATED discovered that its production process for the manufacture of a ceramic product varied with the season. Periods of high humidity adversely affected yield and quality. After extensive study, Corning scientists became convinced that this seasonal variation was the cause of the problem, and they took steps to accommodate this fact.

* THE IBM CORPORATION introduced its System 360 series of computers in 1964.[1] The computer's logic circuitry consisted of a hybrid integrated circuit module containing several silicon chips. A complex metallurgical alloy was developed to serve as the contact between the chip and the substrate. Each chip was coated with a thin layer of glass, adding additional complexity to the manufacturing process. After IBM rapidly increased production of the system, serious reliability problems appeared, caused by corrosion and poor adhe-

---

1. Emerson W. Pugh, Lyle R. Johnson, and John H. Palmer, *IBM's 360 and Early 370 Systems* (Cambridge, Mass.: MIT Press, 1991).

sion of the metal contacts. These failures were traced to the design of the process and the equipment used to scale up production. IBM solved the problem but was forced to postpone further deliveries of the system by as much as four months, the first such delay in IBM history.

Although all three of these defects were eventually removed, they were serious enough to lengthen the product cycle. Could they have been anticipated and prevented? In retrospect, both Abbott and Corning believe that they might have prevented their problems if they had asked more questions and searched more intensively for the answers. In Abbott's case, efforts are now made to ensure that raw material specifications are understood by vendors. Of course, hindsight is always clearer than foresight. Even industry leaders like these three, with the best skills and strong research and development organizations, cannot guarantee that these subtle, insidious technical problems will not occasionally occur. But without the strong technical foundations these companies have built for their products, the defects could have been far more frequent and severe. Companies with a weaker technical base could be severely damaged by such difficulties, and they have less capacity to recover from them.

How does a company achieve a strong technical foundation and how does it apply it effectively to the development of new products? There are three questions that can lead to the answers:

1. Who builds the foundation?
2. How is research integrated into the product cycle?
3. How much research is needed?

Who Builds the Technical Foundation?

The research laboratory is usually the source of the knowledge that builds this technical base. There are really two different classifications of research: basic or "pure" research, and applied research. Basic research is considered scholarly or scientific investigation. It is the source of new technological concepts and new physical phenomena. Although it takes a long time—sometimes years or even decades—before this type of research bears fruit in the form of new products, it is the engine that drives industrial progress. However, applied research—also called product-oriented or process research—is at least as important. It is the work that yields the basic technical knowledge essential to the development of manufacturable and marketable products. Applied research establishes the technical foundation for new products and greatly enhances their chance for success by becoming a direct and continuous partner in the product cycle.

The great corporate research laboratories such as Bell Telephone's Murray Hill, IBM's Yorktown, RCA's Princeton, and GE's Schenectady have been major forces in U.S. post–World War II industrial success. But only the largest corporations can afford mega-research laboratories with thousands of well-trained professionals, hundreds of millions of dollars worth of state-of-the-art equipment, and spectacular campus-like buildings. In fact, only the largest U.S. corporations can afford *any* research laboratories.

Yet every manufacturing enterprise must have access to the basic technical support its products need. There are many opportunities for companies to ally themselves with the expertise that will provide this indispensable assistance. Some companies may be able to afford small laboratories and a few specialists with technical skills essential to their specific product lines. For those that cannot, there are directories listing thousands of companies ranging from large research institutes to one- or two-person mom-and-pop consulting operations that specialize in metallurgy, optics, programming, chemistry, mechanical design, electrical engineering, and many others. This vast capability can be tapped to good advantage. There are many universities and private research institutes possessing a wide range of technical capability in all the physical sciences. One such laboratory is the David Sarnoff Research Center of Princeton, New Jersey, which is devoted primarily to applied research in solid-state physics, consumer electronics, materials sciences, and communications. This laboratory does contract research for both military and commercial products. A case study in Appendix B discusses this organization and highlights some of the opportunities and challenges that exist for companies to capitalize on the power of this type of research organization. Using an outside research laboratory such as Sarnoff entails a number of barriers that must be overcome, including the difficulty in building mutual trust between the laboratory and its customers and gaining ownership of the research results. The ultimate measure of the success of the relationship is the degree to which the customer incorporates the research results into its new products.

How Is Research Integrated Into the Product Development Cycle?

If applied research is a major component of the process of moving products more effectively and rapidly through the product cycle, then it must be closely linked with the other organizations participating in the cycle. Unfortunately, this type of research, if it exists at all, is often completely detached from the management of the product cycle and the engineering and production arms of the company. The connection between research and the rest of the cycle is often so fragile that research exerts little if any influence on the ultimate success of a product.

Today's modern technology gives rise to products composed of intricate combinations of mechanical, electrical, metallurgical, chemical, or optical elements. As a result, the design of the product, the composition of the materials, the processes required to fabricate the product, and the equipment necessary to make it become part of a highly complicated system of interdependent parts. Furthermore, it is almost certain that this trend will increase and even accelerate in the future.

In order to design a reliable and manufacturable product encompassing this system, the researcher, the product designer, and the manufacturer must have a profound understanding of the behavior of the materials and processes used. It is the researcher's job to understand these elements and pass that knowledge on to the designer and manufacturer— and this cannot be accomplished by handing them a set of technical reports or conducting an occasional seminar. It requires a lengthy, continuous, and intimate collaboration.

Part of the problem in achieving the necessary collaboration is the fact that in most U.S. corporations, research scientists, design engineers, and manufacturers live in separate worlds. They practically never attend the same meetings, read the same publications, or participate in the same conferences. In the traditional organization, the research laboratory is treated as an enclave physically and organizationally remote from the product designers and the manufacturing plant, encouraging this polarization. There is also a certain technical caste system in U.S. corporations: Research scientists consider themselves an elite group with a somewhat higher status than development engineers, who in turn consider themselves superior to manufacturing engineers. It may be difficult to convince research scientists to redirect their efforts toward product- and process-oriented research because of their long-held belief that this type of work is less challenging and creative than "pure" research. Furthermore, they may feel that they are losing the freedom that usually exists in a research laboratory if they must work in a more structured environment. In the past, when most manufactured products consisted of simple mechanical or electromechanical assemblies, this state of insularity did not much matter. In the new age of jet aircraft, microprocessors, space exploration, high-performance automobile engines, and large-scale circuit integration, the separation of the scientist from the product designer and the manufacturer can seriously cripple product development.

The need for this new alliance between research, development, and manufacturing is spreading to an increasing number of industries. Table 5-1 illustrates several products, some specific requirements that the product design must satisfy, and the type of technical knowledge that must be obtained before these requirements can be met and the product design completed. In each case, a basic understanding of the properties and control of chemistry and materials must form the basis for the design and production process. In every instance, lack of this knowledge would adversely affect every part of the product cycle. This type of weakness results in marginal product designs, poor process control, low yields, extensive redesign, and longer product cycles.

Table 5-1.

Product/Technology	What We Need	What We Must Know
Auto engine	Better emission control	Properties, control of nev combustion processes catalysts, lubricants
Copier	Copy speed, quality	Toner paper properties, interactions
Electronic package	Strong chip bonds to circuit board	Structure, behavior of complex metallurgical systems
VLSI chip	Lithography for 1 micron features	New tools for high optics resolutions; high sensitivity polymers
Ink jet printer	High-quality print	Properties, control of ink chemistry, paper coating, and interactions
Medical diagnostic instruments	Accuracy, versatility, speed of response	Chemical interactions of reagent, plasma, test container

Of course, it is impractical to delay product development until every piece of scientific knowledge is available. Practically every major technology is exploited commercially long before all the technical uncertainties are eliminated and every scientific phenomenon is understood. If this were not the case, we would not have the personal computer, the space shuttle, or the fuel-efficient engine. A great deal of technological and industrial progress has been made by extensive experimentation and development through empirical means using design-of-experiment techniques. Nevertheless, relying solely on these methods is dangerous. A strong technical and scientific foundation, though never perfect, is essential to shorter product development cycles. Not only is this type of applied research a prerequisite to the design process, it is essential to provide the underpinning of the entire product cycle, and to reduce the program risk to an acceptable level.

Once researchers gain the technical knowledge through

extensive study and experimentation, it must become part of the product design process. The research engineers must be an integral part of the organizational team that is designing and developing the product and preparing for its introduction into manufacturing. The researchers' contributions include:

- Transferring the technical knowledge from the research process to the design and manufacturing engineers
- Working with the design and manufacturing engineers to ensure that the technology or new product concept is technically sound and ready to be designed and commercialized
- Working with the design and manufacturing engineers in identifying the limits of the technologies so that the product can be designed safely within these limits
- Assisting the design engineers in the product design process by interpreting their theoretical and experimental work
- Setting up new experiments and building new laboratory models to gain more knowledge as the product development process progresses
- Studying the behavior, composition, and structure of critical materials and processes and applying the results to the design process
- Developing the new measurement techniques and leading-edge production equipment that will ultimately be required in the new product

Can research be successfully integrated? An increasing number of companies, including the three discussed below, are beginning to carry out this integration with considerable success (see case studies in Appendix B for additional discussion). These companies have recognized that there is a strong relationship between the technical foundation for their products and their ultimate design and manufacturability. They have jettisoned old and obsolete organizational methods in favor of aggressive moves to realign and integrate their operations.

∗ THE DUPONT MEDICAL PRODUCTS AND IMAGING SYSTEMS DIVISIONS have almost completely decentralized their technical activities. Except for a small central research group, most of their research and development has been dispersed to manufacturing sites. Consequently, at each location DuPont has created a total product organization that performs the entire product cycle from research to manufacturing. DuPont has also broken down many barriers to achieving a high degree of integration, including:

- Blurring the lines between applied research and development—the term *applied research* is not even used
- Linking the R & D group and the manufacturing engineers through the use of teams
- Removing the distinction in levels of skills between the research and development staff on the one hand and the manufacturing engineers on the other
- Calling all members of the technical group "the technical community" to further reduce the distinction between the two groups

✳ CORNING GLASS has centralized practically all its technical activities, including research, development, and manufacturing engineering, at one location in Corning, New York, under one organization called the technology group. This organization performs the entire spectrum of activities from research through the development of the manufacturing process before the product is transferred to a manufacturing location. The linkage between research and development, engineering, and marketing occurs through product-oriented teams with membership from all these groups.

✳ THE KODAK COPY PRODUCTS DIVISION has instituted an organizational model quite similar to those of Corning and DuPont Medical Products and Imaging Systems. Previously, the division had distinct and separate research, development, and manufacturing organizations. It has now integrated research and development under one organization. It carries out new product development by using the team concept, with the direct involvement of manufacturing engineering. This integrated operation remains under the management of research and development until the program moves to the production stage. At that point, much of the operation is transferred to the manufacturing organization to complete the transition to routine production.

All three of these examples demonstrate alignments that bring the research laboratory organizationally much closer to the product design and manufacturing parts of the company. These examples are indicative of the importance these companies place on the marriage of science and technology to the design and manufacturing process. Yet these organizational measures are not really revolutionary. Forty years ago, under the leadership of Dr. Jack A. Morton, the Bell Telephone Laboratories pioneered the 416B microwave triode, the basis for the continental radio relay network that brought transcontinental telephone and television to the United States. Bell also converted the invention of the transistor into commercial reality, a development that led to the integrated circuit. Morton was a strong advocate of the premise that applied science and engineering were major elements of the total process of running a business. He championed the concept that innovation should run the gamut—invention, design, development, introduction, manufacturing, and production. In his book *Organizing for Innovation,* Morton discusses the "spatial barrier" that existed in the 1930s and 1940s between the Bell Telephone Laboratories in Murray Hill, New Jersey, and the ten geographically dispersed Western Electric manufacturing plants. To eliminate these barriers, Bell set up laboratories at each of these plant locations. "As a result, the interaction and tradeoffs between design and process, and between cost, reliability, and performance, can be tackled jointly by Bell Labs and Western Electric people with minimum delay, right from the start, at all levels of organization. Mutual education, understanding, and respect grow daily at such an interface."[2]

Companies that are attempting to integrate research into the product development cycle are experiencing varying degrees of success in involving manufacturing in this new alliance. The necessary technical competence must be built in

2. J. A. Morton, *Organizing for Innovation* (New York: McGraw-Hill, 1971), p. 65.

manufacturing, so that it will be on an equal footing with research and development. Some companies complain that because manufacturing engineers often have multiple assignments across many product lines, it is difficult to maintain stable membership on teams and sufficient job continuity to ensure the necessary coordination and communication. These are important problems that companies must solve if this form of integration is to be successful.

How Much Research Is Needed?

One of the most critical moments in the life of a product program occurs when management must decide whether sufficient applied research has been completed, whether a strong enough technical foundation has been built, and whether the time has arrived to commit funds and engineering design resources to proceed to the next step. According to several of the companies interviewed for this book, there is always a certain amount of tension and contention between the research staff, design engineering, and marketing concerning the readiness of a new idea to be converted to a product. The researchers insist that they are not yet prepared to unveil the new technology or product concept and want to hold on to it longer; the marketing group is champing at the bit because they see exciting commercial opportunities; the design engineers are eager to get their hands on it and start work. With greater company integration, this tension may actually increase, since research becomes a more visible and active participant in the decision making.

The most important part of the decision-making process is determining whether a technical basis for the product has been established. The problem lies in the difficulty in finding absolute proof of such a basis. In order to reduce the program risk to a prudent level, there are two questions that company management must answer:

1. What type of research is needed to establish the technical foundation?

2. What type of information is needed to prove that the foundation has been sufficiently built in order to justify investing in the next steps of a product program?

The nature of the research support a company needs in order to design a new product will vary by product and technology (see Table 5-1). For example, an engine manufacturer needs to understand how to prevent oxidation and corrosion; a chemical producer must develop products that are environmentally safe; an airplane propeller supplier must master the properties and behavior of metals in order to build products capable of very high stress; an integrated circuit producer must maintain extreme control of submicroscopic contaminants; and so on. All these requirements demand a strong understanding of the physical sciences. In most industries, and for all but the simplest product or the smallest incremental improvement, the product design must be based on the latest technical and scientific knowledge. The magnitude of the research program for achieving this knowledge depends on how profound the changes involved in the new product are.

The following is a five-step approach to determining the type of applied research needed to provide the necessary technical foundation for a product:

1. Identify and classify the critical and unique features of the new product that will provide a competitive advantage; these features may be a new subsystem, a change in materials, a novel component, or a manufacturing process.
2. Evaluate the degree of change or advance that each of these features represents from the previous product model or generation (see Chapter 4).
3. Estimate how much experience the company and the industry has had with each advance.
4. Determine the technical knowledge that exists to support each advance within or outside the company.
5. Institute the type of applied research program needed, based on the information gathered from the above steps.

Although these steps may appear obvious, many companies either give too little emphasis to them or overlook them altogether. The reason can be traced to the lack of linkage between the research laboratory and the engineering and manufacturing areas. Because of this gap, research either does not recognize the need to support the product designers and manufacturing engineers or is not motivated to do so. In addition, the engineers often overestimate their ability to develop products without research's assistance. And higher levels of management do not understand the technical issues sufficiently to see the need to make applied research a partner in the product cycle.

These five steps are essential prerequisites to any new product strategy, and they take a great deal of study, expertise, and management judgment. The knowledge gained by this type of assessment will tell management what it needs to know to determine whether the program is based on a sound technical footing, or what it needs to do to achieve one.

Are there any dangers in moving research so close to the engineering and production parts of a company? If research laboratories become more deeply involved in the product development process, is there a danger that the character of research will change? Does this mean that research scientists will take over the jobs of product designers or invade the factory floor and become production expeditors? It is up to company management to make sure they do not. The traditional independent role of research to study new scientific phenomena and to discover new technologies must not be compromised. But research needs to add a new dimension. The products and technologies of the present and the future require an increasingly stronger technical and scientific foundation. Research must provide that foundation and become a major partner in achieving shorter product cycles and high-quality, competitive products for U.S. industry. Many U.S. companies are recognizing this fact and taking bold steps toward research integration.

Chapter 6

Integrated Product and Process Design

Product design shares the spotlight with customers as one of the two linchpins of a corporation's entire business (see Figure 6-1). Product design defines the performance, cost, and quality of a product, and it is a major factor in determining how long customers must wait for delivery. If this key element of the product cycle is executed well, the prospects for a successful product in the marketplace increase dramatically. Yet despite its overarching importance, many companies give it too little emphasis, and there continue to be many problems in its implementation. In order to gain a perspective on product design and to demonstrate how it fits into the critical path of the product cycle, this chapter discusses:

- The objectives of product design
- What is wrong with the way U.S. industry implements it
- How engineering changes affect the product cycle
- The importance of integrating product and process design
- The role of design tools in the product cycle
- The steps to take to accomplish integrated design
- How to evaluate the effectiveness of a product design process and how to improve it

Figure 6-1. Integrated design process.

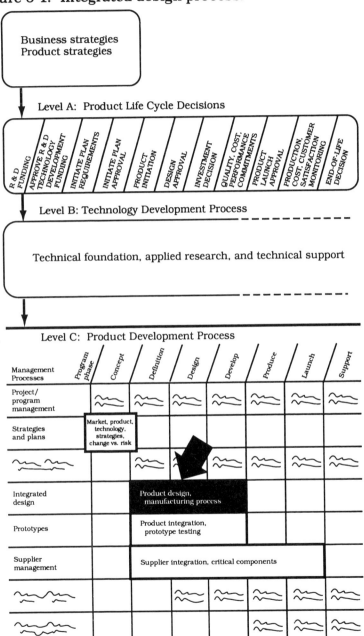

The Objectives of Product Design

Product designers have a pivotal role in a corporation, and their responsibilities are enormous and comprehensive. Consider what they must accomplish:

- The overall architecture of the product
- A complete description of the physical, mechanical, electrical, and chemical content of the product
- The choice of materials, components, and subassemblies that make up the product
- The physical relationships, interfaces, and interconnections between the components and subsystems
- Dimensions and tolerances of the components
- The specifications and performance requirements for each element as well as the total product

To meet these design needs, designers are faced with a number of major technical challenges that are central to the ultimate performance and reliability of a product. For example, a designer of products in the pharmaceutical, chemical, or electronics industry would need to be sensitive to environmental and toxic waste disposal regulations; a manufacturer of automobiles or airplanes would require materials with high stress capabilities; a developer of precision machinery would have to meet the needs of close mechanical dimensions and tolerances; and a designer of integrated circuits must learn how to reduce the presence of submicroscopic contaminants. Designers must not only adhere to product specifications and technical requirements, they must also prove that such parameters can be achieved under high production conditions.

Consequently, a key tenet of this and practically every other book on this subject is the need for a close and interactive relationship between those who design the product and those who develop the manufacturing process. This interaction is vital if the design is to be converted into a high-quality, manufacturable product. In order to achieve these objectives, the process of product design must entail a continuous and lengthy series of trade-offs and compromises between the physical and performance specifications of the product on the one hand and the manufacturing process on the other. This sequence must continue until a satisfactory design that will meet the customer demands for performance, cost, and quality is achieved.

When we think of manufacturing processes, we must consider much more than mechanical or chemical processes, parts standardization, and the mechanical handling and movement of parts. The manufacturing process extends to the architecture and layout of the manufacturing plant, methods of process control, means of protecting the environment, plans for mechanization and automation, information systems, and even employee and customer safety.

All these categories of processes have one characteristic in common: Each influences and is influenced by the product design. This close relationship dictates the need for a strong linkage between the design and the development of the means of reproducing it on the factory floor.

Product Design: What Is Wrong With the American Way?

One of the principal differences between American and Japanese companies is the manner in which this design-manufacturing linkage is managed. A professional colleague of mine, on a trip to Japan, asked his hosts how Japanese companies managed design for manufacturability. The Japanese were quite puzzled by the question. They have no program by that name, and the reason is clear: The ability to expedite a product to market with good performance at low cost and high quality is implicit in good design. The Japanese do not separate these issues into separate departments with different labels, staffed by different people, because they are inseparable. This concept is institutionalized by the Japanese work culture and management style.

The opposite continues to be true in much of U.S. industry. In many companies, the design of the product and the development of the manufacturing process are isolated from each other. The functional organization endemic to most corporations promotes this division between these two highly related parts of the design process, and since management does not always understand the importance of this relationship, it sees no need to make any structural changes.

This separation has also been reinforced by the way most companies reward their product designers. Historically, company management has measured the performance of design engineers solely on their ability to achieve the highest product performance. Although good designers are not oblivious to the importance of cost and manufacturability, they are naturally motivated to put the greatest emphasis on performance because that is what they are paid to do. Automobile designers strive to achieve the highest performance measured by good handling, comfort, safety, styling, and fuel efficiency. Computer designers concentrate on obtaining the highest speed, the most memory with the best access time, and the greatest physical compactness. When these objectives are pursued separately from the manufacturing process, manufacturability takes a backseat in the design process, and the result is higher costs, poorer quality, and longer product development cycles.

Other problems have weakened U.S. companies' performance in product design. There is a lack of sufficient design skills resulting from inadequacies in our educational system. As a result of a National Research Council study, Dixon and Duffey point out that there is little U.S. research in the field of engineering design, and in the approximately 250 engineering schools in the United States there are practically no courses taught in product design. Worse still, they point out, is the fact that there are few people who are even qualified by their experience to teach modern-day design methods.[1]

Consequently, our obsolete organizational structures, our measurement and reward systems, and our inadequate technical skills are all barriers to good product design. It is no wonder that the way we manage design is having a major impact on the length of the product cycle and the quality and cost of our products.

---

1. J. R. Dixon and M. R. Duffey, "The Neglect of Engineering Design," *California Management Review* 32, no. 2 (1990).

The Engineering Change Syndrome

The upshot of all these weaknesses in the way we manage product design is the rapidly escalating number of engineering changes required late in the product cycle. Often this avalanche occurs after the product has moved to the factory floor, into the showroom or store, or even inside the home or on the highway—precisely the time when the frequency of these changes should be declining rapidly. Most companies plan for a certain number of changes, but the actual number they experience is usually far greater and much later than they anticipated (see Figure 6-2).

There are three prevalent types of engineering change problems:

1. A poor system for administering and controlling engineering changes
2. Avoidable and trivial engineering changes
3. Unavoidable and major engineering changes

Each of these categories is the result of different causes, and all of them can have a devastating effect on the length of the product cycle.

Figure 6-2. Engineering changes.

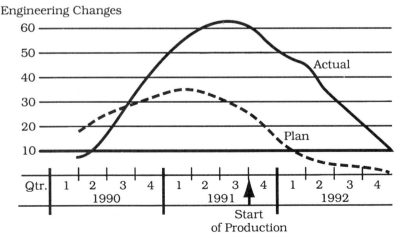

The Engineering Change Control System

Engineering change is not an indicator of failure. In fact, many changes are inevitable, even desirable, in a rapidly advancing and highly competitive industry. Discovering, diagnosing, and instituting the changes necessary to solve problems are part of the design and learning process. But an excessive number of changes, particularly if they happen late in the product cycle, is a symptom of a poor product design. They increase product cost and lengthen the product cycle. Often, the adverse effect of engineering changes is exacerbated simply because a company has no formal system for recording, tracking, approving, and expediting them. This lack of control can cause an upward spiral of problems that can have a severe impact on the program schedule.

Even some highly regarded companies struggle with primitive methods of managing engineering changes. At one manufacturer of automobile components, the entire process of administering changes was accomplished manually, and there was no standard form that could be used to record and monitor them. The changes originated from the design engineer, the purchasing department, the manufacturing floor, the marketing organization, or the quality operation. There was no system for placing them in any time or priority sequence. One clerk tried heroically, but unsuccessfully, to make some order out of the chaos. It often took months, even as long as a year, for a change to be implemented. In many cases, engineering change requests were actually lost, never to be seen again. And some originators of changes put intensive pressure on the clerk to expedite their changes. As a result, so many changes were given top priority that attempting to move them through the clogged system was virtually impossible.

Avoidable and Trivial Engineering Changes

A high percentage of engineering changes can be classified as "avoidable": They occur because of inaccurate materials specifications, poor instructions to the manufacturing workers, or errors on the design prints. Many are caused by poor quality control and a general inattention to detail. Some are technically simple, such as a different label on a container or a new identifying color.

The chaos created by too many avoidable changes and the lack of a disciplined system to control them are both serious product cycle roadblocks, but they are easy to fix. Stronger management, better quality control, replacing paper and pencil with a computer, more attention to detail, and a formal change-control system will go a long way toward solving these problems. But these are not the most serious factors that hamper the progress and add to the length of the product cycle.

Unavoidable, Major Engineering Changes

The greatest threats to the success of product development, particularly in the case of leading-edge products, are changes necessitated by profound and fundamental problems that are difficult to diagnose and overcome and take a long time to solve. They can be traced to weaknesses in the company's management of the key parts of the development cycle.

Often the origin of major changes is far back in the design process, for example, a material that contains unwanted contaminants, a hidden failure mode, a manufacturing tool that was improperly designed, or an assembly of parts that is too costly and difficult to reproduce consistently. In some cases, the source of engineering changes can be traced all the way back to the research laboratory, where the technology had not been sufficiently developed, and unexpected defects did not appear until much later in the development cycle. Many such problems go undiscovered in earlier parts of the product cycle because the methods of simulation and analysis of prototype models were too superficial. Because many of the flaws are caused by fundamental weaknesses in the way the product cycle has been managed, they cannot be removed overnight. The price of these engineering changes is lengthy redesign, long product cycles, high costs, poor quality, and even program failure. Several examples of these types of problems were described in Chapter 5.

There are other consequences of the poor linkage between

the design of the product and the manufacturing process. The following represent experiences of real companies and the problems that resulted from designing the manufacturing process independent of the product design:

∗ COMPANY A management launched a new product line that required a separate factory. In order to expedite the planned schedule, Company A built the shell of the factory at the same time as it began to design the product. In order to design such a shell, some assumptions were made about labor productivity; the type and number of factory tools needed; the work flow; electrical, gas, chemical, and water distribution systems; the number of workers and other personnel required to operate the factory; and the expected market for the product. Building the shell well in advance of its need appeared to be a wise and farsighted decision. In principle, it was, but its execution created some serious problems. As the development of the product proceeded and as the manufacturing process and equipment were designed, it was discovered that all the earlier assumptions about the ingredients of the factory were wrong. Furthermore, it seemed that the market potential for the new product line was much greater than had originally been assumed. There was no way that the factory Company A needed could be squeezed into the shell. The result was a physically fragmented production line, a less efficient work flow, a longer development cycle, and higher costs.

∗ COMPANY B manufactured automobile transmission parts. A new product it was introducing appeared to be quite simple in design. It consisted of a metallic plate to which a fibrous material would be bonded with a polymer. In order to cut costs and raise its market share, company management decided to build an automated production line to perform the assembly operations as well as the high-temperature bonding process. Since Company B did not have the internal technical capability to develop automation equipment, it subcontracted development of the equipment to an outside supplier. When the production line was installed, Company B engineers soon discovered that it simply would not work. Yield of good product was low, the equipment was constantly breaking down, the throughput of the line was a small fraction of expectations, and the quality of the few pieces that finally emerged from the end of the line was poor. The reason: The design of the product, the bonding process, and the automated tools were completely incompatible. The equipment was eventually scrapped. This disaster occurred because Company B underestimated the process complexity of the product and maintained little linkage between the design of the product and the development of the manufacturing process, as well as with the vendor that actually developed it.

The third example describes a much less expensive mistake, but it also illustrates the importance of the design-process linkage.

✳ In the late 1960s, many automobile models incorporated a small vent window in the left front door that was separate from the main window and adjustable by a crank handle. In that design, there was a metal channel at the top of the door that wrapped around the window when it was fully cranked. That channel also assisted the technician who was assembling the door to guide the glass into its uppermost position. One year, one of the Big Three auto manufacturers eliminated the vent window on one of its models. At the same time, the design engineers eliminated the metal channel, forgetting the role it played in the assembly process. To assist in the assembly of the window into the door, engineers designed a machine mounted on an overhead trolley that would attach the window with a series of suction cups used to help the technicians guide the window into position during the assembly process. A technician who performed this process told me that it was extremely cumbersome. As the car moved down the assembly line, he had only one and one-half car lengths to do the job, less than half the time he needed. There simply was not enough time to pick up several parts associated with the assembly, fumble with the window, and complete the entire process. The only way the technician could perform the window assembly satisfactorily was to enter the car and manually insert the window as the automobile continued down the line. After a series of Band-Aids, a less costly and more permanent solution was finally instituted twelve months later.

Integrating Product and Process Design

The integration of product design and the manufacturing process is one of the major keys to shortening the product cycle, and the traditional functional organization is poorly equipped to do so. Departmental insularity, adversarial relationships, and top management remoteness are all barriers to bringing about the necessary cooperation, unity, common sense of purpose, and intensive communications and synergy required for successful integration. Consequently, major changes in organizational relationships are urgently needed. Many U.S. companies are beginning to take some limited steps in this direction.

Concurrent Engineering

The most popular label to describe a method of bringing product design and the manufacturing process together is "concurrent" or "simultaneous" engineering. Concurrent engineering is often defined as the means of carrying out the engineering process by forming a team whose members come from many disciplines, including marketing, product design, manufacturing engineering, quality control, and purchasing. The normal activities of product design and development of the manufacturing process are carried out in parallel rather than in series, reducing the time it takes to perform both tasks. Many of the companies I studied are trying to institute concurrent engineering, and volumes of published books and articles have discussed it. But despite widespread attempts to practice this form of engineering, there are problems in implementing it and in fitting it into the overall company strategy and culture. How can it be made to work?

First, design and manufacturing engineers must do more than carry out their tasks in parallel. In order for manufacturing engineers to begin to develop the manufacturing process and plan the manufacturing plant, they need to be in constant communication with the design engineers so that they understand the state of the design at every point. Working in parallel is not enough. There must be a constant dialogue.

Even that exchange of information is not sufficient. As the design engineers begin to design the product, the manufacturing engineers must make judgments concerning the manufacturability of the design and how it will influence the characteristics of the process, the tools, and the makeup of the production floor. If the manufacturing engineers determine that the design presents serious problems in cost or manufacturability, they must work with the design engineers to resolve these problems through a series of trade-offs that may well involve changes in the design itself. The two groups must develop an intensive working relationship that goes well beyond parallelism—their activities must be integrated. Clark and Fujimoto have discussed in detail how this intensive relationship is working in the Japanese automobile industry.[2]

But to make concurrent engineering really work, this integration must involve more than design and manufacturing engineers. The team must include representation from every critical area in development and production, including the purchasing department and the direct labor force. If the product involves the purchase of components or subsystems, the concurrent engineering team must include the direct and intensive participation of suppliers. They must be as much a part of the integrated design process as the engineers from within the company (see Chapter 8). If the new product contains major advances in technology and product features, participation must extend to the applied research laboratory. The technical knowledge that results from research becomes the foundation for this stage of the cycle; the product design process builds the structure of the product on this foundation.

2. Kim B. Clark and Takahiro Fujimoto, *Product Development Performance: Strategy, Organization, and Management in the World Auto Industry* (Boston: Harvard Business School Press, 1991).

It is very difficult to determine at what point research ends and the product design phase begins. In fact, depending on the magnitude of the product advance, research may never cut the umbilical cord that ties it to the product cycle until there is absolute assurance that the product is manufacturable, marketable, reliable, and competitive. In the case of a mature product, or one that involves only small incremental improvements from the previous one, that cord has likely been cut a long time ago. But, as we discussed in Chapter 5, in a new, competitive, and constantly advancing product line, research must continue to be an active participant in the product cycle. That is why many companies are uniting their technical activities covering the entire span from research to manufacturing, both organizationally and geographically.

Ultimately, the success of concurrent engineering depends on how a company defines and uses it. If it is applied narrowly as a means of pursuing design and manufacturing operations in parallel, with manufacturing playing a subsidiary role as a "student," the approach will be much less effective. If it is broadened to include the direct, participatory, and contributing role of all the important parties from research to the suppliers, concurrent engineering can be the vehicle for achieving integration of product design. In order to broaden the concept, I refer to it as *integrated design*.

Integrated Design

In addition to using cross-functional teams, many of America's leading companies are beginning to recognize the defects of the old and outmoded organization and to favor new structures that lead to greater integration of design and a broadening of organizational scope to include the manufacturing process. Many larger companies are decentralizing their operations and dividing them into business units, each containing its own marketing, research, development, and in some cases even manufacturing functions. The case studies of Abbott Laboratories, DuPont Medical Products and Imaging Systems, and Kodak Copy Products in Appendix B describe how these companies have pursued this type of decentralization and integration.

There are an increasing number of examples of successes in integrating the product design and manufacturing process:

＊ In 1985 the RCA CONSUMER ELECTRONICS DIVISION developed a new color television chassis, with the goal of a thirty-month product cycle—considerably shorter than its usual process.[3] RCA appointed a strong leader to direct the project and, with the assistance of United Research, formed a series of "natural work teams" with product design and manufacturing engineering participation. These teams addressed every aspect of the design and the manufacturing process. This new venture into concurrent engineering presented many organizational and cultural problems, but they were successfully overcome. By integrating the product design and the manufacturing process, RCA cut its normal product cycle by more than 50 percent.

The power of integrating product design with the development of the manufacturing process is illustrated by these examples.[4]

＊ TEKTRONIX learned to assemble its 11400 series of oscilloscopes in forty-five minutes, compared to nine hours for the less complex 7854 predecessor.

＊ With the addition of only one part, VOLKSWAGEN designed its automobiles so that the front end could remain open while the engine was installed by a hydraulic arm. This installation, which formerly required several men and one minute, now requires one robot and twenty-five seconds.

There are many examples of the application of Design for Manufacturing and Assembly methods and software devel-

3. Daniel Valentino and Bill Christ, "Teaming Up for Market: Cheaper, Better, Faster," *Management Review,* November 1989, pp. 46–49.
4. Daniel E. Whitney and Charles Stark, "Designing for Producibility, Manufacturing, and Design—A Symbiosis," *IEEE Spectrum,* May 1987, pp. 47–54. Copyright 1987 IEEE.

oped by Boothroyd-Dewhurst, Inc.[5] If these tools are used early in the product design process and are integrated with the design, they can result in significant reduction in costs and increase in design and assembly simplicity. For example:

* TEXAS INSTRUMENTS—reticule assembly—reduced the number of parts by 75 percent and assembly time by 85 percent.

* FEDERAL PRODUCTS CORP.—column gauge—reduced the number of components by 25 percent, cost by 20 percent, and assembly time by 15 percent.

* DIGITAL EQUIPMENT—computer mouse—reduced the number of operations from 83 to 54 and assembly time from 592 seconds to 277.

* FORD MOTOR CO.—transmission assembly—reduced the number of parts by 20 percent, the number of operations by 23 percent, and labor minutes by 29 percent.

These are all impressive results of the use of integrated design. They demonstrate the potential of coupling the design of the product with the development of the manufacturing process. These methods have been particularly valuable in parts assembly processes and when smaller incremental changes from product to product are involved. But in the case of more dramatic advances in technology and product complexity, the use of design for assembly methods and integration of the designer and manufacturing engineers are but two of many steps companies must take to bring about significant improvements in cost, quality, and product cycle time.

Potential Problems

Despite numerous examples of success of integrated design, there are also many problems. First, companies often continue to be entrenched in the old mode of engineering and manufacturing separatism. This mentality explains their reluctance to involve manufacturing engineers at stages of the development of a new product; they believe it is financially

5. *DFMA Insight*, Boothroyd-Dewhurst, Inc., 1991.

risky to do so until the design work is sufficiently advanced to permit productive manufacturing activity.

Even if management supports the concept of integration, merely making the manufacturing engineers members of the team is not enough. Integration can succeed only if all of the parties have equal status. The iterative nature of the dialogue that must take place in order for each participant to contribute and directly influence the ultimate product design requires mutual respect, shared goals, common experiences, and equivalent technical strength. To foster this equality, the company must acquire and train manufacturing engineers who have the same level of technical competence and stature as their research and development counterparts and are compensated with equivalent pay. They should also have comparable experience so that they can understand both the process of product design and its implications to manufacturing.

Unfortunately, these conditions of equality rarely exist. Consequently, manufacturing has difficulty attracting the more gifted engineers, who naturally gravitate toward those activities they perceive as more prestigious and rewarding. But some companies are recognizing the problem and taking steps to solve it. For example, at DuPont Medical Products and Imaging Systems there is little distinction in the technical training and skill levels among the research, development, and manufacturing engineers who work together on product introduction teams. The title Manufacturing Engineer does not even exist. All these professionals are referred to as the "technical community."

A further impediment to the effective use of integrated engineering is the lack of continuity among team participants. The management of many of the companies I studied complained that they had difficulty maintaining a stable and continuous manufacturing representation (see Chapter 10). Although research and development participants were usually dedicated to one program and stayed with it on a permanent basis, qualified manufacturing engineers were frequently in short supply and were often spreading their efforts and time across many assignments. This team instability and constant shifting of people greatly hampered the effectiveness of the program.

The Design Tools

No discussion of product design would be complete without some mention of such design and technology tools as CAD/CAM (Computer Aided Design/Computer Aided Manufacturing), statistical process control, Taguchi methods of experimental design, DFA (Design for Assembly), and CIM (Computer Integrated Manufacturing). In the past, these methods have been highlighted in many publications as the principal solutions to low productivity and long development cycles. More recently, there has been less enthusiasm for these methods. In the Gemini Consulting interviews with twenty-one professors at leading U.S. business schools (see Appendix A), there was a consensus that these tools have been oversold, poorly used, or misapplied. The results of the Gemini Survey of 200 company executives were equally surprising. Less than 5 percent named these types of tools as their top priority for investing in the future. (See Appendix A for a detailed review of these studies.)

Why has there been such disenchantment with these tools? Have they really failed? For an answer, look at the results. Although CAD/CAM is still in a relatively early stage of development, and research will undoubtedly continue to enhance its capability and power, it is already becoming an indispensable tool. It is incomprehensible that industries such as automobiles, electronics, and machine tools would be able to survive without it.

The application of statistical process control and Taguchi experimental design has spread rapidly and has greatly advanced the state of product design and quality control. Clearly any company would profit by capitalizing on these important methods.

The use of computers in manufacturing has spread like wildfire. No modern company could perform data collection, inventory and production control, testing, materials requirements planning, process control, or even the payroll without computers.

All these tools have reached an advanced stage of development and have proved themselves useful. We are continually learning how to utilize them. As a result of a collaborative industry-university study, Boston University professor Stephen Rosenthal describes in detail methods for selecting and implementing these design tools.[6] Then why all the gloom about their alleged poor performance and pessimistic predictions about their future? The reason is that despite their success and even indispensability in performing many tasks, they have not yet succeeded in playing a major role in improving overall productivity or competitiveness. No matter how technically advanced these tools are, and regardless of the high level of skill of the people who use them, they will not, *by themselves,* significantly advance our competitiveness because our foreign competitors have the same tools. In addition, such tools do not constitute a force that attacks the basic problems in product development, nor are they *alone* a part of the critical path that determines the length of the cycle. Nevertheless, these technology tools and techniques are essential parts of the solution. When properly used as components of a total strategy, these tools will reinforce and enhance the integrated design process. Like the violin to the violinist or the microscope to the research scientist, these are the essential tools of U.S. industry.

Integrated Design: How Do You Do It?

Now let us summarize the steps that must be taken to do integrated design right.

1. Treat the product design and the development of the manufacturing process in a unified, integrated manner.
2. If the product contains significant advances in design complexity, design features, materials, or technology, make research a close partner in the product cycle.
3. Carry out this process with a team of the best technically trained research, development, manufacturing,

6. Stephen R. Rosenthal, *Effective Product Design and Development: Cutting Lead Time and Increasing Customer Satisfaction* (Homewood, Ill.: Business One Irwin, 1992).

and purchasing representatives with comparable stature and ability.

4. Form the team early in the product cycle, assign a strong leader, give the team all the authority it needs to do its job, and keep it intact with a minimum of turnover in its membership.

5. Identify the critical areas of concentration that are essential to achieving a competitive and manufacturable product design and give them extra emphasis. These critical areas will, of course, vary by company, industry, and product line.

6. Invest in the most advanced design tools appropriate to the products.

Accomplishing each of these steps is no trivial matter. Changing the company culture to break down the barriers between functions, generating continuity of team membership, elevating manufacturing to the position of equal partnership, and raising the technical level of manufacturing engineering all require major revisions in structure, behavior, and employee and management measurements and rewards. But assembling teams and instituting concurrent engineering methods under today's conditions are not enough. Much more profound institutional change is needed to make a lasting impact on the length of the product cycle. The executives I interviewed from companies that are attempting to adopt these measures expressed their concern about the difficulties they were encountering. But that is all to the good. Recognizing barriers to progress is the first step toward removing them.

Evaluating and Improving Integrated Design Programs

The following guidelines are intended to help you evaluate the strength of your integrated design program as well as identify the steps you can take to strengthen it or to develop one. With the knowledge you have about your own industry, you are the best judge of your ability to meet these guidelines.

If you are satisfying them, and if you have dedicated the right skills and capital resources to carry out this work as part of the early product design stage, you have taken a major step toward achieving a successful integrated design.

Human Resources

☐ *Engineering capability and skills: Do these characteristics fit your company?*

1. Design and manufacturing engineers have equal levels of skills, academic training, work experience, and capacity for innovativeness.
2. Design and manufacturing engineers are judged by the same standards, receive comparable levels of pay, and are given comparable levels of responsibility.
3. All engineers, both design and manufacturing, represent a wide range of disciplines appropriate to the product, including mechanical, electrical, chemical, metallurgical, and optical.

☐ *Engineering teams: Do you have them, and is this the way they function?*

1. All members have equal status and are considered equal contributors.
2. All members serve from the beginning to the end of the design cycle.
3. All members serve permanently and are totally dedicated to the achievement of integrated design.
4. The human relationships are sufficiently developed to promote effective teamwork.
5. The members have been trained properly to work in a team environment.

Product Design and Manufacturing Process

Are you implementing the following type of work on the manufacturing process, if appropriate for your product, early and as an integral part of the design?

☐ *Design for simplicity*

1. If the proposed design of the product is too complicated for economical manufacturing, and if there
   are so many parts with complex motions and interactions that the design will create cost and reliability problems, determine what design changes can be
   made to reduce the complexity.
2. Determine whether the number of steps in the processing of a part or component can be reduced by
   eliminating some steps or combining others, and
   whether alternative processes can be developed to
   make these reductions without changing the product performance specifications.

☐ *Materials and processes*

1. Identify the most advanced design and process features of the product, how much of an advance from
   previous products these features represent, and
   what experience exists with them under manufacturing conditions.
2. Determine the technology limits of the design and
   how close to the limits of temperature, physical
   stress, metal fatigue, and electrical breakdown the
   product will operate with the anticipated design
3. Determine what must be known about any new materials that will be used, including their availability, composition, chemical structure, toxicity,
   environmental problems, and limits of use (e.g., low
   and high temperature, mechanical stress, insulating properties, electrical breakdown, shelf life).
4. Determine what new and untried manufacturing
   processes must be developed, the technical challenges in using them, and gaps in knowledge about
   them.
5. Determine what measurement techniques exist to
   characterize new materials and processes and what
   new techniques must be developed.

☐ *The manufacturing facility*

1. Study the overall concept for an architecture of the
   manufacturing line of the new product.

2. Determine how much automation versus manual assembly will be used and the type of automation needed, and perform an economic analysis to justify the approach.
3. Develop a plan for work flow, logistics, and equipment layout philosophy (e.g., serial versus parallel, use of process centers).
4. Identify unique environmental controls, clean-room concepts, special material handling, toxic waste disposal, safety methods, and so on.

Chapter 7

The Prototype: The Product Integrator

Deeply embedded in the first stages of development of a new product are many invisible flaws that must be discovered before that product can eventually be converted to manufacturability and marketability. Unless these problems are located, diagnosed, and removed, the product cycle may extend indefinitely, and the prospects for success will be poor.

A principal instrument for searching for these latent problems is the *prototype* (Figure 7-1). A prototype is an original form or model on which later stages are based or judged. Continual testing of prototypes of the total integrated product as well as its individual parts is a major factor in achieving shorter cycles and top quality. The National Aeronautics and Space Administration (NASA) learned this lesson the hard way.[1] During the building of the Hubble space telescope, James Beggs, the head of NASA, discussed with his staff the possibility of more extensive testing of the fully assembled telescope, but such testing was dismissed as unneeded. The assumption was that such a test would yield no information that could not be gained through separate tests of the primary and secondary mirrors. Although some optical experts questioned the wisdom of this decision, Beggs defended his policy before a July 1990 Senate hearing chaired by Senator Barbara Mikulski (D-Md.). So NASA launched the telescope—with disastrous consequences: The images sent back to earth

1. "NASA Head: Hubble Tests Dismissed," Gannett News Service, *Poughkeepsie Journal,* 19 July 1990.

Figure 7-1. Prototypes.

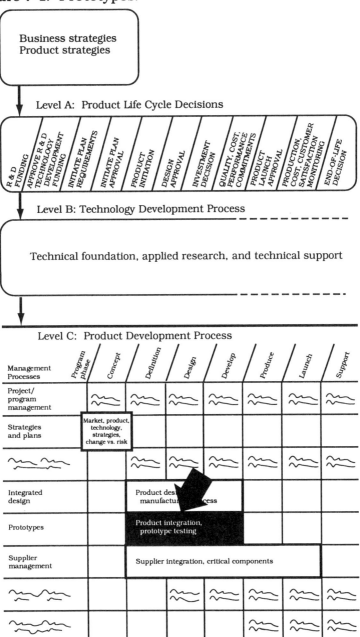

were blurred and virtually useless. It may be surprising that a highly esteemed agency such as NASA would make this kind of blunder, but even the best and brightest sometimes lose sight of simple basic truths.

The only conclusive way to determine whether a product concept is sound, the technical base is strong, the design is workable, and the total integrated product operates as a working system is to build a prototype and test it. During the development of a new product, the prototype is the reference point from which the value of future improvements can be assessed as product development progresses. Of even greater importance is the use of a prototype to search for and detect "invisible problems."

Paradoxically, early program success can actually become a trap. Those who have participated in research and development will recognize the following scenario: Early prototypes actually work the first time they are assembled. Yields in the laboratory are unexpectedly high, and management is in a state of euphoria. Press releases herald the new breakthrough that will revolutionize the industry. Then reality sets in. Yields plummet, new and troublesome defects appear, and many months pass before the initial success is repeated. Such instant success is usually an illusion, and if management misinterprets its meaning, the program will most likely be destined for serious trouble.

Companies often gloss over or even ignore danger signals during the early part of a development program, only to find out too late that serious problems suddenly erupt like a volcano. The reason they discover these problems so late is that they never looked for them in the first place! The situation is similar to that of the patient who claims that except for some minor symptoms, which obviously are not serious, he feels good. Therefore, he never goes to a doctor, never has a physical examination, then suddenly has a heart attack. This process of denial applies to companies as well as individuals. Understandably, management does not enjoy hearing bad news, but in product development, if it does not listen to bad news and take corrective action at the beginning of a program, the later news will be much worse. Every program manager who begins to launch a new product should assume that invisible problems exist and bend every effort and expend whatever resources are necessary to find, identify, diagnose, and solve them as early as possible.

When complex product systems are involved, subtle and unexpected problems can arise even after extensive testing and apparently successful operation for an extended period of time. The story of the Traffic Alert and Collision Avoidance System (T-CAS) is an example. In 1989, the Federal Aviation Administration (FAA) ordered that most commercial aircraft be equipped with a system that warned of approaching airplanes so that pilots could take evasive action. But, according to a story in *The New York Times,* "Air traffic controllers around the country say phantom images of other planes often appear on airliners' cockpit computers. The latest incident occurred last Thursday, when the pilot of a United Airlines flight approaching O'Hare International Airport here tried to avoid a plane that was not really there."[2] Although the FAA and the traffic controllers' union disagree about whether this problem causes a safety hazard, this is just another example of the difficulties of achieving perfection in complex systems containing an intricate marriage of hardware and software.

How to Use Prototypes

The value of testing prototypes depends on when they are built and how they are used. If prototypes are tested late in the product cycle, it will probably be too late to correct any problems that are revealed without serious consequences to cost and schedule. If prototypes are used solely to prove that a design "works," even if they operate near their specifications, their value is minimal. The ultimate potential of prototypes will be realized only if they are used as analytical, diagnostic, and corrective tools. The value of prototypes depends directly on the timing, frequency, and intensity of their use.

Although they may not approach the complexity of the Hubble telescope, T-CAS, or a space station, most manufac-

2. "Air Controllers Say Computers Show False Images," AP, *The New York Times,* 21 April 1991.

tured products on the market today, from home appliances to computers, from garden tractors to automobiles, from floppy disks to silicon integrated circuit chips, are complex systems of software and hardware consisting of assemblies of highly interrelated combinations of mechanical, electrical, electronic, metallurgical, chemical, or optical elements. Because of the complex interrelationships and interactions between and among these parts, and because these interactions are difficult to define, characterize, specify, and measure, it is virtually impossible to build an operable, reliable, and reproducible product at a competitive cost the first time a product is assembled. The reason? It cannot be accurately predicted how all the variables in all the pieces of the product system will behave as part of the total product until a vast amount of data and experience during operation of the system are accumulated. Sometimes these invisible and unpredictable flaws do not occur during early tests. Often they suddenly appear, then disappear like a meteor, leaving no clue as to why they came and why they went.

The process of discovering and solving problems during the product development phase consists of a lengthy series of steps involving constant designing, building, testing, diagnosing, and redesigning. Even the best-designed products go through an extended journey of trial and error. Take, for example, the Patriot missile, which, though still somewhat controversial, proved its worth in the recent Gulf War. "When the Patriot missile system was first fielded, its radar went haywire 'whenever the wind blew,'" recalls former Reagan defense official Lawrence Korb; it took three years to work out all the bugs.[3]

Prototypes clearly play an important role in the product development process. They are the best indicators of how far you have come, where you have to go, and how you will get there. If used correctly, prototypes do far more than indicate success or failure. They provide priceless information concerning the mistakes made, the reasons for them, and the direction to take to correct them and proceed with development.

3. Stephen Budiansky with Bruce B. Auster, "A Force Reborn," *U.S. News and World Report,* 18 March 1991.

The more frequently prototypes are used, and the more thoroughly and rigorously they are studied, the greater the probability that the program will stay on the right track and succeed.

The Number of Prototypes

There is no magic formula for calculating the optimum number of prototypes a program will need. The manufacturer of a component such as a spark plug, a silicon chip, or an oil filter may need to build hundreds, perhaps thousands, of prototypes to prove that the design can be manufactured with uniformity and high quality. The producer of a copier, a personal computer, or a garden tractor may be able to prove the soundness of the product design with ten or twenty prototypes. An aircraft manufacturer may be able to gain invaluable information with only a few prototypes that are constantly modified with each new change as the program evolves. Each company must make a trade-off between the number of prototypes that will yield a statistically valid level of data and the cost. The engineers will fight for numbers that they consider a necessity; the controller will in all likelihood brand these costs prohibitive. Top management will eventually make the decision. When making that decision, management must recognize that the prototype, if it is used in strategic parts of the product cycle and is applied as an analytical tool, is a key to shorter and successful product development, and that a prudent investment in it is not a luxury but a necessity.

As with any investment decision, management must strike the right balance between the costs involved and the benefits achieved. Simulation is one way of reducing the cost.

During the early development stage, simulation is a powerful engineering tool for evaluating the product performance likely to occur in actual operation without building physical hardware. The science of simulation has greatly advanced in the past ten years. For example, International TechneGroup Incorporated has developed computer simulation tools that have been successfully applied to significantly shorten the product development cycle and reduce product cost. It achieves these results by accelerating the study of alternative product designs and manufacturing processes as well as determining the best match between them.[4] As a result, both the expense of building prototypes and the length of the prototype cycle have decreased for many new product designs, particularly those involving relatively small, incremental design improvements. But when more sizable changes are involved, and when there are many unknowns in the design and process, the usefulness of simulation is limited. For complex assemblies and structures in which the interactions are not sufficiently understood or are not predictable, controllable, or measurable, simulation will not adequately predict performance under different operating conditions. In these cases, the building and testing of prototype hardware are essential. Nevertheless, simulation should be used as much as possible to reduce the need for the costly and time-consuming building and testing of prototypes.

There are other ways of minimizing the number of prototypes without diminishing their effectiveness as diagnostic tools. The first is to build prototypes only at certain critical points of the product cycle. Or, depending on the product, the same prototypes can be used for each stage, substituting only the most critical and advanced parts of the prototype or modifying only parts of the prototype as development progresses. One aircraft company minimized costs by using airframes from twenty-year-old planes as the basis for its early prototypes, then retrofitting them with the new and most critical components and design features of the new aircraft.

The Timing of Prototypes

One of the keys to the success of prototypes is to test the entire product as well as the individual pieces. Each part of the product system may work well individually, but the total system may not work at all. The most critical prototype test occurs

4. Jason R. Lemon, *Concurrent Product/Process Development,* Transactions of Users Conference, Information Services Conference Dentsu, July 1988.

near the beginning of the design cycle, or possibly earlier. If a product consists of a complex assembly of interactive parts, the earlier you assemble all the parts, test their behavior as a total system, determine whether it works, look for problems (you will have little difficulty finding them at this early stage), and diagnose them, the faster you will learn and the shorter the product cycle will be. Eastman Kodak's Copy Products Division, a manufacturer of copiers, formerly delayed its first total integrated product prototype until late in the product design phase. However, it paid a high price in the length of its product cycle, because problems that could have been revealed by testing prototypes much earlier cropped up too late to solve them in time to meet its schedules. As a result of this experience, Kodak now builds its first integrated prototype very early, even before the beginning of product design.

If prototypes are built early and at critical phases of the development cycle, and if the information derived from testing these prototypes is obtained quickly enough for the engineers to respond rapidly with design improvements, the length of the development cycle can be reduced dramatically. Faster response time in building, testing, and modifying prototypes is one of the factors that gives Japan a significant lead over the United States in product cycle time. In an analysis of lead time for building prototypes in the automobile industry, Clark and Fujimoto found that the prototype lead time in Japan averaged 50 percent of that of U.S. and European manufacturers. They attribute this differential to the fact that Western firms place less emphasis on time as an important aspect of the prototype process.[5] My experience in other industries, including electronics, confirms this lack of attention. In fact, the primary reason that prototypes take too long to build, and are built too late to be effective, is that management simply gives them a low priority, either because it does not understand their importance or because it is reluctant to make the necessary investments.

Figure 7-2 shows the critical steps of the model testing

5. Kim B. Clark and Takahiro Fujimoto, *Product Development Performance: Strategy, Organization, and Management in the World Auto Industry* (Boston: Harvard Business School Press, 1991), p. 196.

Figure 7-2. Stages of model testing.

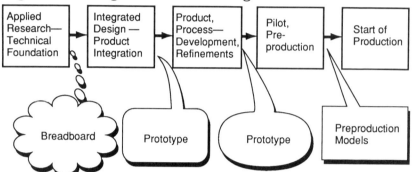

cycle. A prerequisite for moving from one step to the next is the successful completion of the previous step. A prototype is the vehicle for proving that each step has been completed satisfactorily. Table 7-1 lists the tests that should be made at each phase and what information should be obtained from them.

The Character of Prototypes

Because the nature and objectives of a prototype will change at each stage, its purpose must be well defined. The prototype built to demonstrate feasibility of the product concept or a new technology is often called a *breadboard*. Due to the early stage of development, it is sometimes relatively crude in construction, and its purpose is to demonstrate the feasibility of operation of the individual parts of the system as well as to verify certain principles. It is often used to determine how to satisfy some basic requirements such as choice of materials. For example, before Kodak could build a breadboard of a new model copier, it needed to locate a supplier that could make a transfer roller with the necessary electrostatic and conductive properties.

As the design cycle proceeds, the character of the prototype changes. As soon as possible after the breadboard is assembled, the complete integrated product should be built in order to identify the total design and any problems that arise

Table 7-1.

Program Phase	What to Test	What to Study
Applied research, technical foundation; breadboard	Individual subsystems, total system breadboards if possible	Feasibility of concept, feasibility of technology, key problems, readiness for design stage
Product design, manufacturability; prototype	Individual subsystems and total integrated system	Design, system, process problems; ultimate manufacturability
Product, process development; prototype	Individual subsystems and total integrated system	Performance of integrated product; remaining design, process, systems integration, and manufacturability problems; reliability
Pilot or preproduction	Total integrated product	Final proof of manufacturability, product performance, reliability, shippability

because of interactions between the individual components. During the later stages of product and process design, the prototype should not only prove that the product performance requirements will ultimately be met but demonstrate that the product will be manufacturable. When pilot production begins, the design of the product should be nearing completion and the manufacturing process should be well developed. Thus, the product model that comes off the pilot production line should no longer have the character of a prototype. Of course, there will continue to be modifications and fine-tuning of the design and the process, but the model should be very close to the ultimate, shippable product. If too few prototypes have been built, or if the prototype test and analysis have been too superficial, the problems that should have been discovered early on will show up in pilot production—with adverse consequences for the length of the product cycle.

Table 7-2 compares Japanese, American, and European automakers and the average number of prototypes per body type, then compares the number of pilot vehicles built before production begins. Note that although all the countries studied build approximately the same number of body-type prototypes, Japan produces far fewer pilot models. Clark and Fujimoto interpret these data to mean that "each Japanese prototype is a more powerful problem-solving tool and that product and process designs are consequently much more complete when they reach the pilot line."[6] By placing major emphasis on a strong technical and design foundation for their development programs, the Japanese greatly accelerate the learning process and reduce costly manufacturability and quality problems as they build up their production.

What Prototypes Do for You

Prototypes are indispensable tools for measuring progress, speeding up the learning process, and ensuring the success of

Table 7-2.

	Japan	U.S.	Europe Volume Producers	Europe High-End Specialists
Engineering prototypes				
Total	82	44	73	61
Per body type	38	34	37	54
Pilot vehicles				
Total	120	192	233	218
Per body type	53	129	109	205

Source: Kim B. Clark and Takahiro Fujimoto, *Product Development Performance: Strategy, Organization, and Management in the World Auto Industry* (Boston: Harvard Business School Press, 1991), p. 196. Reprinted by permission.

6. Clark and Fujimoto, *Product Development Performance,* p. 196.

a new product program. They are also the major tools for accomplishing several other objectives:

• Evaluating complex materials, process, and equipment interactions; these interactions may be impossible to understand because they are in the realm of art, not science, but prototypes demonstrate what will and will not work.

• Determining what changes in the product and process design must be made and assessing how these changes will work; although many changes can be attributable to poor workmanship or poor engineering, many are unavoidable consequences of the development learning process, and the faster the changes are made, the shorter the learning cycle.

• Proving that the design and process are well within the limits of the technology.

• Proving that the design is manufacturable.

• Detecting, diagnosing, and removing serious failure mechanisms.

• Proving that the product will function under conditions of stress and determining limits of operation under these conditions.

The Prototype Cycle

There is far more to using a prototype than assembling the parts and throwing the switch to see if it works. To exploit its full potential, it is essential to follow a series of well-defined steps:

1. Use simulation as much as possible.
2. Build the prototype.
3. Perform extensive testing under electrical, mechanical, and physical stress.
4. Determine whether it is operating to specifications.
5. Identify defects, failure modes, and performance problems.
6. Search for hidden, subtle problems.
7. Describe the characteristics of these problems and determine their origin.

8. Implement design changes to fix the problems identified.
9. Retest the prototype after implementing all design changes.
10. Repeat the entire sequence until all problems are solved.

The performance of these tasks requires that management place a very high priority on the prototype program and commit enough engineering resources to make it work. The problems that are identified by these tests are not necessarily trivial. The engineering work that these tests may dictate can be as intense and challenging as the research and development that resulted in the building of the prototype itself. Throughout the development cycle, prototype testing may reveal major design flaws and unsuspected failure modes, and may even raise serious questions about the viability of the technology itself. That is why extensive testing of prototypes is important and must be carried out as early as possible. This principle applies to any product in any industry.

Figure 7-3 demonstrates why the speed of building and testing prototypes is so critical in expediting the development cycle. Figure 7-3(a) shows a development program in which two sequences of prototype building and testing are planned. Each sequence is planned for twelve months and is divided equally among the first product design, building of the prototype model, and evaluation of the model. In actual practice, these three activities most likely are not—and should not be—carried out in series, since in most cases they are not separate, discrete events. As testing progresses, many changes will be made to the model, which will be constantly retested. At the end of the first twelve months, design changes will be made to correct problems revealed by the evaluation of the first prototype. The new design modifications will be incorporated into the second prototype, which will also pass through a series of evaluation tests. At the end of the twenty-four-month period, assuming the success of these evaluations, the design is considered ready for preproduction and subsequent entry into manufacturing.

Figure 7-3(b) depicts a more probable result of the plan

Figure 7-3. The prototype cycle.

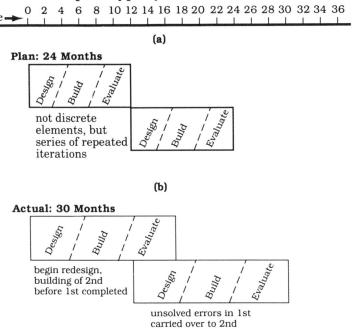

(a)

Plan: 24 Months

not discrete elements, but series of repeated iterations

(b)

Actual: 30 Months

begin redesign, building of 2nd before 1st completed

unsolved errors in 1st carried over to 2nd

shown in Figure 7-3(a). Instead of the planned twelve months for the first sequence of designing, building, and testing, the entire process takes eighteen months. Why? Because of delays caused by the excessive turnaround time to build the prototype, evaluate it, feed information back into the design process, and then incorporate the necessary changes into the prototype model. These delays are often due to poor management commitment and low priority as well as insufficient resources applied to the prototype process. The many design iterations that may occur during the prototype cycle just add to the length of this time and greatly extend the product cycle. As a result of these delays, management, in its haste to expedite the lagging program, begins building the second prototype before the evaluation of the first one has been completed. But the second prototype cycle becomes even longer than the first, and the program slips even further. Since the unsolved problems of the first model are most likely still embedded in the second prototype, engineering changes increase, and the program continues to slip. The principal lesson to be learned from this example is that the faster the turn-around time in building, testing, and diagnosing problems in the prototype, the shorter the product cycle. In fact, the length of the product cycle is practically proportional to the length of the prototype cycle. Clark and Fujimoto state that their "evidence suggests that a one-month reduction in prototype lead times results in a one-month reduction in engineering lead time."[7]

The Do's and Don'ts of Prototype Use

The following examples illustrate the value of intelligent use of prototypes in carrying out the product cycle as well as the problems created by poor management of their application.

Successful Prototypes

* THE AIRCRAFT COMPANY designs, assembles, and markets military and civilian aircraft. As is typical of moderate-size companies in this product line, it designs and subcontracts to outside manufacturers all components and subsystems, including engines, airframe, and all the electronics and navigational systems. Then it integrates and tests the assembled aircraft. Safety is obviously of overriding importance. That is enough of a reason to place the prototype tests at the head of the list of essential elements of the product development cycle. Aircraft Company built its first prototypes very early in the cycle. Its engineers not only rigorously tested the airframe and the total integrated system to prove that the new model plane would fly, they also savagely tested individual components. They left no stone unturned when looking for those invisible problems that could later have very serious consequences for passenger safety. Using specially built equipment for testing, they bent the ends of wings repeatedly, literally thousands of times, until the wings broke. They performed this drastic and destructive testing procedure for the purpose of locating, diagnosing, and removing unknown failure mechanisms in the material and wing design.

7. Clark and Fujimoto, *Product Development Performance,* p. 182.

In addition, they repeatedly raised and then dropped the entire airplane to the ground from a height of six feet to test the reliability of the landing gear under extreme stress. They conducted these tests long before the first production model was built and the first passengers were safely flown to their destination. This company went far beyond simply proving that the plane would fly. It used its prototypes as analytical and problem-solving tools.

✳ In the early 1970s, the program manager of the new IBM System 370 computer, which was then under development, assumed that a long stream of unpredictable problems would eventually rise to the surface as the development program progressed. Most of these problems were likely to occur in the logic circuitry, which would be the principal building blocks of the mainframe of the computer. In order to expedite this discovery process as early as possible in the product cycle, IBM designed an automated production line to fabricate the silicon circuit chips.[8] The major objective of this line was to build these chips rapidly for use in development prototype computer models so that changes to the design of the chips as well as the computer models could be made rapidly. In essence, both the chips and the computer models were prototypes that could be quickly designed, tested, and redesigned if necessary. The use of this "quick turnaround time" prototype line greatly expedited the product development process of the silicon components as well as the entire computer system and was a major contributor to IBM's success with this product.

The following is an example of the poor use of prototyping by a major U.S. company developing a leading-edge product.

Too Little Prototyping

✳ The concept for the product and technology to be used was developed by the company's applied research laboratory. The product consisted of several subsystems that would be

8. William E. Harding, "Semiconductor Manufacturing in IBM, 1957 to the Present: A Perspective," *IBM Journal of Research and Development,* p. 647, September 1981.

linked together into a total system. Near the conclusion of the research program, the research engineers built and tested a breadboard model to determine whether it worked. Unfortunately, it did not: The individual parts of the system had been developed separately by different research groups, and when they were finally assembled for the definitive test, the total system simply could not function. To make matters worse, there had not been enough analytical study to determine why the system would not work.

Despite this failure, company management, in its haste to meet its committed program schedule, began the product design of the system. After a considerable amount of design work had been carried out, approximately one year before the product was scheduled to be manufactured, a second prototype was built. The testing of this model confirmed the results of the first prototype: It still did not work. In order to expedite the program, engineering management sought funds to build several more prototypes—more than it had originally planned. It was hoped that such an intensified testing program would breathe some life into a failing project.

The schedule was seriously slipping, and costs were skyrocketing. Top management denied the funds engineering had requested and, further, ordered that the number of prototypes be *cut* to combat the increasing program costs. But further reductions in these prototypes would clearly contribute to further deterioration in the program. The company was caught in a vicious cycle. The failure to solve the problems revealed by the first research prototype and the delay in building the second prototype until the date for manufacturing began to loom ominously ahead both contributed to the inevitable schedule delay and cost escalation. Yet the cure for the ailment was more of the same: Cut out more prototypes. Ultimately, the company was able to build an operable model, but only after costly program delays and loss of market share.

Planning a Prototype Program

Here are some guidelines to use to plan a prototype program and measure its effectiveness:

1. Identify the critical points in the product cycle where achievement of the following objectives must be proved:

   • The basic technology used in the product is feasible.
   • The basic concept of the product is sound.
   • The total integrated product operates successfully.
   • Design flaws, systems integration problems, and reliability defects are identified.
   • The initial design of the product will eventually achieve satisfactory performance to the required specifications.
   • The product design will ultimately be manufacturable, reliable, and serviceable.
   • The manufacturing process will reproduce the design successfully in large-scale production.
   • The design and the process have reached a sufficiently advanced stage of development that investments in factory tools should be made.

   Several stages of prototypes may be needed to prove that all these objectives have been met, but in some cases more than one objective can be proved in one stage (see Figure 7-2).

2. Use the most advanced simulation tools available to the limit of their capability.

3. Determine the appropriate types of tests that must be performed to evaluate each objective, including tests to evaluate:

   • Performance of the prototype compared to the design specifications
   • Performance variations while modifying operating conditions
   • Performance under extreme electrical and mechanical stress as well as environmental conditions of high or low temperature or humidity

4. Develop analytical tools to diagnose physical problems such as surface contamination, metallurgical failures, insulation breakdown, metal fatigue, structural weaknesses, or other phenomena that are relevant to the particular products and technology.

5. Set up a process for rapidly communicating test findings to design and manufacturing engineers so that they can analyze the results, quickly modify the product design, and continue the process of design and development.
6. Support all these steps by persuading top management to give the prototype program a high priority and enough resources to carry it out.

This type of analysis will help you evaluate the state of the prototype program and assist you in making the necessary changes to strengthen it. But you should exercise some caution in the use of prototypes. Prototypes should not become a substitute for sound engineering or a crutch to prop up a weak product program. Every effort should be made to reduce the number of prototypes by using simulations and emphasizing a strong product design program. But there are times when the building, testing, and analysis of hardware are essential.

The prototype must be an integral part of the product cycle, and it must be given a high priority by management and the commitment of enough resources to ensure that the prototype cycle is carried out as rapidly as possible. The prototype is a major building block in the product development process, and if it is applied strategically and intelligently, it can contribute substantially to a shorter and successful product program.

Chapter 8

The Supplier: A Partner in the Product Cycle

So far we have been discussing successful integration within the corporation. Now we need to look at how to integrate operations that take place outside the company (Figure 8-1). Virtually no company today manufactures all the components that go into its products itself. In fact, a large part of a company's manufacturing goes on outside its walls. For example, in a review of the MIT study of the worldwide automobile industry, Womack, Jones, and Roos state that the 10,000 parts of a typical modern automobile are manufactured by at least 1,000 to as many as 2,500 companies.[1]

This fact provides management with a convenient excuse when its company's performance lags behind. Suppliers get the blame! "We did our part," says company management, "but supplier 1 missed the schedule and supplier 2 sent us a defective part." Yet the factors identified in this book as being critical to the success of the product cycle are as important to the supplier as to the manufacturer of the end product. This means that the supplier must act virtually as if it were a part of the company it serves. And it is up to corporate management to orchestrate a total management system encompassing all the activities carried on both inside and outside the company. If the supplier's performance is unsatisfactory, the manufacturer must share the responsibility.

Achieving the integration of an outside supplier into the product cycle is even more difficult than integrating a com-

1. James. P. Womack, Daniel T. Jones, and Daniel Roos, *The Machine That Changed the World* (New York: Rawson Associates, 1990).

Figure 8-1. Supplier integration.

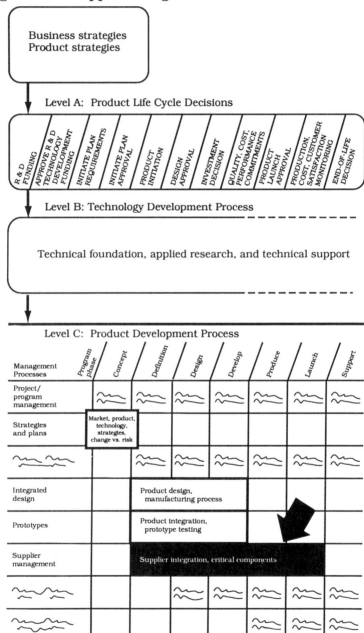

pany's internal operations, and that difficulty increases as products become more complex and industries become more competitive. Yet without this very tight interaction, companies can lose a great deal of control over their destinies in moving new products to market. These close ties may not be very important in purchasing sheet metal or copper wire. But companies buying critical technologies and components are often held hostage to the performance of their suppliers unless they have developed a close relationship with and have a high degree of confidence in them.

In order to understand the role of the supplier in the product cycle and the way companies should manage their relationships with them, we will discuss three issues:

1. How do companies decide what they should buy and what they should make?
2. What are the problems related to buying critical components?
3. How can companies work with their suppliers to solve these problems?

The answers to these questions will have a major influence on a company's profitability. A sound make-or-buy decision and a strong relationship with suppliers will go a long way toward shortening the product cycle and increasing the rate of successful new product programs a company launches.

Deciding What to Make and What to Buy

Some make-or-buy decisions are simple. The purchase of standard commodities may involve relatively short negotiations on price and delivery, and the buyer-supplier relationship is routine. But deciding whether to purchase components that are vital to the success of a product is one of the most crucial choices management must make. In order to explore this issue, I first define what a critical component is.

The manufacturer of practically any product can point to certain parts, components, or subsystems that are pivotal to the design and performance of that product. Vital product elements include the transmission of an automobile, the engine of an airplane, the integrated chip in the computer processor, or the fuser of a copier. They can also be the equipment used to manufacture the product itself. In earlier chapters, the influence of the manufacturing process on the product design was discussed—for example, precision machine tools for fabricating mechanical parts, photolithographic equipment for silicon chips, or robots for performing complex assembly operations. Such process tools are as important to the ultimate performance of the end product as the critical components that go into it. Figure 8-2 shows a simple block diagram of a

Figure 8-2. Critical parts of a product.

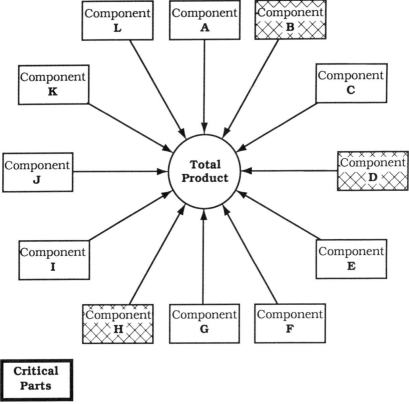

- Pivotal to competitive advantage
- Most Advanced in design, process
- Patent, proprietary position

product made up of a series of components. The components indicated by the crosshatching, B, D, and H, represent critical parts of the system. Critical parts are those that have one or more of the following characteristics:

- They are essential to achieving the desired performance and competitive advantage of the product.
- They contain the most advanced, leading-edge design and process characteristics.
- They are the most proprietary and important to the company's patent position.

How a company manages the purchase of these all-important parts plays a major role in determining the length of the product cycle, the ultimate performance of the product, and even the company's competitive position. The make-or-buy decision is an important part of business strategy, but there is no formula for such a decision that applies to every corporation. Each company is influenced by its own set of business circumstances. However, we can get a perspective on some of the issues that are important in making this decision by reviewing a few examples of how individual companies have approached it. These examples illustrate the make-or-buy strategies of three different companies in three separate industries.

＊ *Buy everything.* An airplane manufacturer buys every piece of hardware that goes into its product. The company designs the aircraft, specifies the performance requirements of each of its components, and then subcontracts everything to outside suppliers, including the airframe, engines, propellers, and communications and navigation equipment. After delivery of these components, it assembles prototypes of the entire plane and carries out an intensive sequence of tests and analyses. This strategy frees the company from making the immense investments in skills and capital resources needed to manufacture the critical parts. It can rely on experienced suppliers rather than undertake the massive problems of building that same capability within the corporation. But despite these advantages, this strategy of total purchasing has several problems:

- Quality-control experts and engineers are stationed near their suppliers and make occasional visits to them. When they are not satisfied with the suppliers' progress, they escalate the issues to top management of both companies. The entire process is agonizingly slow. Since the suppliers are not intimately coupled to the airplane's design process, and since the trade-offs that must take place between the design of the plane and its components consume a lot of time, the product schedule often slips by months or even years.
- Since the suppliers possess the expertise in each of the critical parts of the aircraft, they are in a strong position to influence the plane's design, leaving the aircraft manufacturer at their mercy.
- Unless the suppliers of the key parts of the aircraft invest in major advances in their respective products and technologies, the aircraft company is limited in its ability to advance the performance of its new models. In essence, the suppliers set the pace of the technological progress as well as the competitive capability of the aircraft manufacturer.

This airplane manufacturer markets a safe, reliable product, but it is not a leader in its field. In fact, the company is having trouble maintaining market share. Its purchasing policies are not the only cause for its mediocre performance, but its "buy everything" strategy combined with its arm's-length relationship with suppliers certainly constrain its ability to compete effectively.

✻ *Manufacture most critical components internally.* IBM CORPORATION has adopted a totally different strategy in its use of suppliers. It not only manufactures the entire main-frames of its large computers but produces many of its own integrated circuits, as well as peripheral equipment such as disk drives. In the early 1960s, IBM made a strategic decision to develop and manufacture many of the critical solid-state components to be used in its computers, despite the fact that a successful and well-equipped semiconductor industry already existed.[2]

IBM realized that the semiconductor circuit was critical to the success of its products. Looking into the future, IBM predicted that integrated circuitry would advance in both density and performance to the point where the silicon chip would actually become the computer itself. If IBM were to leave the manufacture of its chips to suppliers, the tail would soon be wagging the dog.

IBM's decision was both bold and risky. It meant that it would need to commit huge financial resources and create a giant organization of new technical skills almost totally different from those of its own computer engineering and manufacturing staff. In embarking on such a major building program, it was also competing with well-established and highly professional semiconductor companies such as Fairchild, Texas Instruments, and Motorola and eventually Intel, Advanced Micro Devices, and National Semiconductor. IBM eventually succeeded in building the largest integrated circuit business in the world, even though it never sold any of its components outside the company. This strategy was an important factor in enhancing IBM's spectacular growth in the 1960s and 1970s and was partly responsible for its leadership in the computer mainframe industry.

* *Selectively manufacture highly critical components.* The middle ground between these two examples is the strategy of manufacturing only a few critical components internally. STANLEY MAGIC-DOOR, a division of Stanley Works (see Appendix B), followed this practice in marketing its swing door system, an automatic door that opens and closes as you enter or leave a supermarket. A major design challenge was to provide a safe zone behind the door so that it opens when you enter but does not slam you in the face as you pass it. The key to this zone is a sensing device that communicates to the door the fact that someone is about to enter. In the past, a sensor was placed under a floor mat. However, a Swedish com-

---

2. Emerson W. Pugh, Lyle R. Johnson, and John H. Palmer, *IBM's 360 and Early 370 Systems* (Cambridge, Mass.: MIT Press, 1991).

petitor developed an electronic sensing system that was so superior it threatened Stanley's market position. As a result of this competitive pressure, Stanley developed a sophisticated electronic system of its own. This product uses an infrared sensor that is controlled by a microprocessor. The sensor sends out information describing a number of discrete infrared zones to an encoder attached to the door. This apparatus continuously senses the location of the door, and it knows what size zone it should generate.

Stanley normally buys most of its components from outside suppliers. But, when pressed by competition, the company made a selective, strategic, and ultimately successful decision to develop and make its own sensing device. Stanley not only obtained patents on this invention, it preserved its market position with a highly successful product.

Which of the three strategies was right? There is no clear answer. These three companies operate in diverse business environments. They represent three separate industries, make totally different products, and are influenced by differing competitive situations. An approach that fits one could be completely wrong for the others. But there are some lessons to be learned from these three examples.

Any company that adopts the "buy everything" mode of the airplane manufacturer must accompany this strategy with a completely different means of working with its suppliers. And this overhaul must extend well beyond the purchasing department. The entire engineering and manufacturing operations must learn how to create such tight linkages with the supplier that both parties are working virtually as one company. The aircraft company in the example did not meet this condition, and it is achieving only limited success in its market.

IBM's totally different approach has, in the past, achieved considerable success. But unless a company possesses the vast technical and financial resources of an IBM, and unless the basis for competition demands it, going as far as IBM can be risky.

Stanley Magic-Door is more representative of a large number of small and middle-size manufacturing companies.

It has succeeded in its strategy of purchasing most of its parts but selecting the most critical and proprietary components for internal development and manufacture.

It may be no coincidence that the two companies that chose to develop and manufacture their most critical components are both leaders in their respective fields, and the "buy everything" company is not. It is also possible that these two corporations could have purchased their critical components and still succeeded—but only if they maintained extremely tight collaboration with their suppliers throughout the entire product cycle. Of course, there are many other reasons that can explain the achievement of leaders and the lackluster performance of the less competitive companies, but the make-or-buy decision as well as the means of carrying it out are important factors in the management of the product development cycle.

The choice of what to make and what to buy cannot be made simply by comparing costs from suppliers' catalogues, particularly when they fall under the "critical" classification. But there are a number of steps company management can take to accumulate the information required to make this vital decision. The first step is to analyze the major components of the product and classify them according to the following four categories, using the "critical" definition discussed earlier in the chapter:

1. *Very critical.* Of overriding importance to product performance, competitive situation, and patent position; a very strong candidate for manufacturing within the corporation.
2. *Somewhat critical.* Important but less critical than the first category; a candidate for internal manufacture.
3. *Not critical.* Generally available with no more than minor modifications; a strong candidate for outside procurement.
4. *Standard, off-the-shelf components.*

The make-or-buy decision for categories 3 and 4 are simple. Standard purchasing agreements and limited contracts may be all that is necessary to buy components in category 3, and buying from a catalogue or the neighborhood hardware store will do the job in category 4. But decisions on the first two categories are more difficult. In order to make them, you need to evaluate these issues:

- Does the capability exist inside the company to design and manufacture the component?
- Which suppliers are capable of developing and manufacturing these components?
- Is there an economic advantage in making the component inside the company rather than buying it?
- What are the competitive and proprietary advantages of making it versus the risks of buying it?

Do not select a supplier based on which is the lowest bidder. There are much more profound issues to study. For example, you should evaluate a supplier's:

- Technical and management strength
- Technical foundation for its product
- Track record on delivery and the types of products it has been successful in delivering
- Capability to do a thorough job of designing, developing, and testing a product
- Willingness and ability to work with your company on an integrated team basis

Once you have thoroughly studied these issues, you will be in a better position to make a decision.

Purchasing Critical Components: The Problems and the Challenges

Once you have decided which components to buy, the next step is to understand the complex relationship that must exist with the supplier as well as some of the problems that can arise if that relationship is too remote. There are essentially two types of problems. The first type can occur because of sloppiness on both sides, particularly the supplier's. Every company has its own share of disasters, such as delivering a chemical with an incorrect label on the bottle or shipping a ton of the wrong size screws. These types of errors can be serious, but they can usually be solved by better production control and distribution systems; they do not require a research laboratory or an integrated engineering team to prevent them.

The second type of problem is far more profound, and it can have a much more serious effect on the length of the product development cycle. These problems occur because manufacturers and their suppliers continue to function in the obsolete mode of separateness and contention. Despite the extreme interdependence between the supplier's component and the end product, the design of each is carried out almost independently. Chapter 6 discussed the complex interactions between the various components of a system and how difficult, yet extremely important, it is to integrate these components into the complete product. This integration is accomplished by making a lengthy sequence of design trade-offs among all the components, resulting in a total product that works. If the supplier of a critical component is not a close partner in this design and integration process, the product can experience major schedule problems and inferior levels of quality.

In many cases, design problems are further complicated by the fact that the supplier may be relying on other suppliers for the purchase of parts to be incorporated in its product. This means that the design of the end product may depend on complicated interrelationships of several parts, all originating from different companies. The following example of the design of engine lubricants illustrates this problem and how it contributes to longer development cycles. This example is representative of the type of complexity entailed in the design process as the number of suppliers involved multiplies.

✳ THE ABC OIL COMPANY sells engine oils to automobile and machinery companies. Its products are critical to the success of its customers. The development of these materials is long and difficult and is complicated by the trend toward increasingly stringent environmental laws. A typical lubricant may entail the mixing of a base oil and as many as six or seven additives. Each additive has a different function, such as the prevention of corrosion and oxidation, improvement of viscosity, or reduction of foam. Marrying these lubricants to the engines they protect is further complicated by environmental requirements and fuel-efficiency standards. The development of these products is lengthy because it requires many iterations in the design of the lubricant to satisfy the needs of the engine. Each iteration involves a repeating sequence of formulation, test, and reformulation.

ABC purchases many of the lubricant ingredients, e.g., the base oil and additives, from several different suppliers. Unless the relationships between ABC and these suppliers are very close, the development of the lubricant can take a long time. Figure 8-3 shows a typical scenario in which the DEF Engine Company orders lubricant from ABC with certain specifications that would result in stringent reductions in corrosion and oxidation. ABC in turn orders the base oil and three additives, each from a separate supplier. Since the characteristics of these constituents are difficult to measure or specify, ABC must formulate the product to determine its performance with a mixture of these constituents. Proof of success can be obtained only by testing the lubricant in the engine built by DEF. If the lubricant fails to meet the engine

Figure 8-3. Engine lubricant supplier interrelationships.

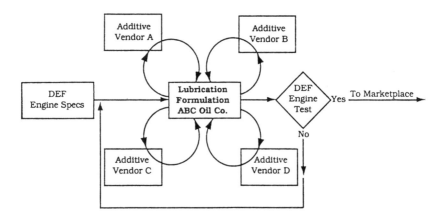

performance requirements, ABC must try another mixture, and this reformulation may require modifications of the additives.

The process of repeating this sequence now involves six companies—ABC, the four suppliers of the base oil and the three additives, and DEF. The length of the cycle to produce an acceptable lubricant will be determined by the number of iterations between ABC and DEF. To further aggravate this lengthy process, ABC may have to negotiate different specifications for the additives it buys. Furthermore, the length of each iteration will be a function of the number of times trade-offs are required between ABC and its four suppliers until it produces a satisfactory formulation to be sent to DEF.

During the development of a new lubricant, the design can be complicated by the discovery of unexpected problems. In the 1980s, to satisfy new exhaust emission standards mandated by environmental control laws, the automobile companies designed their engines so that exhaust gases would be recirculated to reduce nitrogen emissions. After extensive development of new lubricants that satisfied the requirements of this new design, an automobile manufacturer encountered sticking of the recirculation control valve and traced the problem to the lubricant formulation. The manufacturer also discovered oxidation and deposits in the crankcase. The discovery of these new defects in the engine-lubrication system required further experimentation and reformulation until the problems were solved.

The search for solutions to complicated problems like this one is particularly difficult when design trade-offs must be made across several company lines, and it can create major slippages in the product cycle. The delays created in the development of lubricant systems demonstrates the importance of the tightest possible linkage between the manufacturer of the end product and the supplier of critical components.

Is this example unique, or is it an exaggeration of the problem? I believe that it is neither. Consider the examples in Table 8-1 of products and the components that will probably be purchased from outside suppliers. In each case, the supplier will, in turn, buy critical parts from a secondary supplier for use in its component product. In some cases the secondary

Table 8-1.

Product	Component Supplier	Secondary Supplier	Tertiary Supplier
Automobile	Differential	Precision bearings	
Copier	Fuser roller	Rubber, aluminum core	
Automobile	Engine	Electronic controls	Circuit boards, chips
Truck	Engine	Rings, pistons, valves	

supplier may even turn to a third supplier for parts; consequently, the design of the end product involves interactions between several companies.

Another factor that will greatly influence the length of the product cycle is how the supplier of each component develops its product. Many new components represent an advanced state of the art, and the supplier needs to establish technical feasibility, implement a lengthy period of product and process design, and carry out extensive prototype analysis and testing. In other words, the development of purchased parts must pass through the same process of development as the end product.

But there is a difference. The supplier is another company, physically remote, with another work force, a separate management, and even a different culture. Despite these differences, the manufacturer must be certain that the supplier has executed its product cycle successfully and that the purchased component can be satisfactorily integrated into the product.

The Solution: Supplier Integration

If companies are to achieve satisfactory results, they must establish tighter linkage and integration with their suppliers. Many companies are beginning to make moves in that direction. The electronics industry can serve as an example of this trend: Technology and international competition are forcing it in that direction. In fact, there is simply no way to design and manufacture complex electronic systems without this close relationship.

If you looked inside your television set, calculator, automatic garage door opener, home appliance, or burglar alarm system, you would see an assembly of miniature electronic parts that includes silicon chips, circuit boards, and some electrical connectors. If you studied the electronic circuitry of a computer mainframe you would observe the same type of components, except that they would be considerably smaller, far more numerous, and packed much more densely.

In addition to their physical integration, the design and performance of the total product and each of these tiny components are highly interdependent electrically. This means that the design of the total product must be carried out in an intimate alliance with the design of each of its components. Yet there is a high probability that the silicon chips, the circuit boards, and the connectors originate from different manufacturers. Consequently, the design of the electronic product may involve trade-offs between the product manufacturer and the two or three producers of the individual components. Therefore, the design of these electronic products has some similarity to the design of the engine, its lubricant, and the lubricant additives. But the electronics industry is facing up to this fact in a different manner. Electronic product manufacturers and their suppliers are collaborating in the design process from the very beginning of the product cycle.

The case studies in Appendix B include the description of two suppliers of electronic components: Analog Devices, a manufacturer of integrated circuits, and Burndy, a producer of electrical connectors. Both of these suppliers have developed strong relationships with the customers buying their products. Although their executives develop strong bonds with their customer counterparts, much of the coordination occurs between the design and manufacturing engineers of the two parties, who work together on design teams. Because of this close working relationship, they can coordinate and make trade-offs between the design of the components and that of the end product. This intensive interaction begins very early in the design cycle and continues throughout the product cycle. In effect, all these engineers are participating in the design work as though they were members of the same company. As a result, the suppliers have:

- Substantially decreased the cycle times for both their components and their customers' products.
- Learned a great deal about the needs of their customers by working so closely with them—knowledge that will greatly enhance their future business.
- Improved their own product performance.
- Increased the level of confidence and trust their customers have in them.

In turn, their customers have:

- Reduced the length of their product cycles.
- Succeeded in manufacturing higher-quality and better-performing products at lower costs.
- Found suppliers they can trust, as well as a guaranteed flow of high-quality components that work in their products.

This type of supplier-customer collaboration has become an important ingredient in the management of new products in the electronics industry. It is one of the reasons that the Japanese electronics industry holds a position of world leadership. And many other highly competitive and advancing industries would profit greatly by this type of supplier-customer integration.

There are many reasons that some companies succeed and others fail. The supplier relationship is only one of the many aspects of management that contribute to a company's performance. But the trend toward greater technological complexity and product performance, as well as the increasing dependency of most companies on a rapidly expanding base of suppliers, clearly makes the management of this relationship of paramount importance to any company's success. The lessons to be learned are these:

- The integration of the supplier into the product development cycle is a major key to shorter development cycles.
- Top company management must give high priority to make-or-buy decisions on critical components.
- The relationships with suppliers of critical components must be radically changed from the traditional, pro forma, and arm's-length purchasing agreements of the past to close, integrated partnerships.

How can we do it? There is no easy prescription. There are many barriers caused by differences in geography, skills, culture, and objectives that both parties must overcome. Reconciling these differences and making the two companies function as one is a major task. And it will not happen by calling a few meetings or having occasional golf games. But there are a number of measures that a company can take to build the necessary bridges and breed mutual confidence. The responsibility for the first and most important step lies with top management. It must be convinced that forging a strong supplier relationship is of utmost importance. To make that relationship a reality, top management must:

- Stress the need for this integration repeatedly and measure the management team by its success at accomplishing it.
- Build strong links with suppliers at all levels—starting at the top of the company and moving down the corporate ladder to the purchasing department, design and manufacturing engineering teams, and the production line—through constant contact, joint meetings, and sharing of information.
- Integrate supplier engineers into design teams.
- Take suppliers into its confidence by discussing product objectives and design information and generally making them feel a part of and major contributor to the product program.
- Develop a system of rewarding suppliers for good performance.

In the Gemini Consulting surveys, 51 percent of the executives polled rated their suppliers' performance only average. If U.S. industry wants to lead worldwide competition, it will have to do better. Improving this rating is as much a responsibility of the companies that are being supplied as it is of the suppliers themselves. Both parties can take a major step in this direction by making significant changes in their relationships with each other. Making all this happen will require time and a great deal of persistent effort, but it is worth the cost. An effective supplier relationship is one of the key elements on the critical path toward a shorter product cycle, better products, and competitiveness.

Chapter 9

Investments: When Do You Make Them?

The sixth and final element of the critical path to a shorter development cycle is the decision to make capital investments (Figure 9-1). The timing of the decision to acquire manufacturing equipment and build the production plant is crucial to the success of the cycle. And this event is directly dependent on the successful completion of the other five elements. Unless the management process encompassing all these critical components has been carried out intensively and conclusively, making major investments can be a premature step. And since most companies also purchase their most critical pieces of production equipment from outside suppliers, the supplier relationship discussed in Chapter 8 becomes even more important to the length and success of the new product program and further complicates the potential pitfalls involved in these investment decisions.

During the earliest part of the product cycle, a company takes relatively few financial risks. Purchasing equipment for experimentation in the laboratory entails little exposure but presents an opportunity for a sizable payoff in novel product ideas, new processes, and perhaps a major breakthrough invention. Later, building prototypes or a small pilot line entails greater investments, but the risks are still relatively small. But the moment of truth arrives when tens or hundreds of millions of dollars of the company's assets are on the line, and all the promises of the program manager, market researchers, product planners, research scientists, and design and manufacturing engineers must finally bear fruit. If that

Figure 9-1. Capital investments.

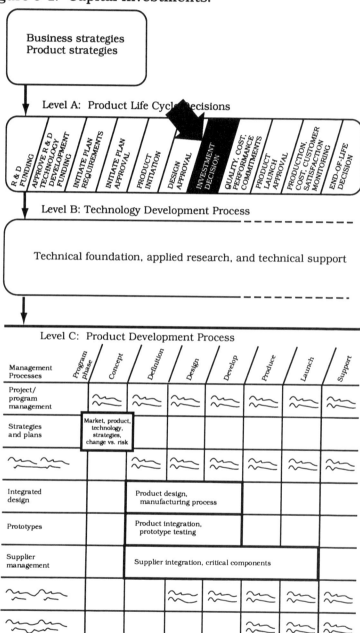

decision is made too early, it can create major schedule delays and cost overruns. If that decision is made too late, the manufacturing capacity will obviously be insufficient to meet the sales forecasts. The challenge management faces is in determining when the right time has arrived.

If a new product entails only a small, incremental advance over the previous one, the decision is relatively simple and involves little risk. The purchasing department and the manufacturing engineers, in conjunction with the suppliers of equipment, determine the lead time for ordering the tools, preparing the factory space, debugging the production line, and starting manufacturing. By adding these estimates of time, they can determine when the equipment must be ordered. The basis for these simple calculations is experience from previous programs. The lead times for delivery of the production equipment are predictable, since most of the tools are probably standard and represent the current state of the art. The performance of the equipment and the manufacturing processes, including tool throughput and utilization, process yields, and worker productivity, are simple to estimate from previous experience. The time needed to debug the process and begin large-scale production can also be predicted accurately based on previous experience. Even determining the layout of the manufacturing plant and the time to prepare it for production entails little difficulty. But in competitive industries, where sizable new product, technology, and process advances are a necessity, it is dangerous to use this simple method of calculation.

The Risks of Premature Investment

Although the risks of ill-considered investments should be obvious, companies often make huge expenditures far too prematurely. It is not unusual for a corporation to commit resources before it has done the homework essential to assure the soundness of the investment. Company A, discussed in Chapter 6, made such premature investments by constructing a poorly designed building to house a new factory before it had developed the production process well enough to accurately specify the design. Company B, also discussed in Chapter 6, made a similar mistake by building an automated production line before it had developed the product and the manufacturing process sufficiently to design the process equipment. General Motors did the same by investing billions of dollars for automation that never worked.

The ramifications of these premature investments can be serious. If the production line is designed and constructed before the product design and the manufacturing process have reached an advanced stage, estimates of yield, labor productivity, equipment capacity, and reliability will be unrealistic. The result will be a manufacturing facility that is characterized by excessive rework, poor yields, low output, chronic bottlenecks, and high work-in-process inventories. The upshot will be higher costs and longer product cycles.

The consequences of premature investment are particularly serious in the production scale-up process. At the beginning of manufacture, as the volume of product increases, the entire production system is under stress. This is the period when personnel productivity is still low, process control is poor, the performance and reliability of the equipment are erratic, logistics problems abound, and many other unpredictable snafus arise. These types of problems are normal in any new manufacturing line; they are a part of the inevitable learning process. But if the product design itself is defective, if the total product system has not been adequately integrated and tested, if the manufacturing process is poorly developed, or if the product is using unproven technology, the scale-up period can be chaotic. The problems of the normal learning period become greatly amplified and uncontrollable. And worst of all, it is often impossible to find the causes of these problems and solve them. As a result, several courses of action may be necessary:

- Make extensive engineering changes in an attempt to keep the production line operating at an acceptable level of productivity.
- Redesign the equipment and the process to increase their capability.
- Add more equipment and rearrange the production line to increase its capacity.
- Scrap the equipment and start all over again.

Each of these remedies would result in increased cost and a longer development cycle. All of them are caused by purchasing production equipment without the essential strong foundation of the other key elements of the critical path.

Timing the Investment Decisions

Like most important management decisions, the timing of these investments involves a combination of technical competence, quantitative data, qualitative judgment, experience, and a willingness to take prudent risks. Figure 9-2 shows two alternative means of carrying out the product cycle—serial and integrated design—and the relationship of investment decisions to them.

The first method, shown in Figure 9-2(a), is the outmoded serial approach. In this illustration, we move from left to right in a temporal progression as the design and development activities proceed. As illustrated in the diagram, the product design is carried out separately from and before the development of the manufacturing process. Then, when the process and equipment development have been completed, some form of pilot production proceeds with whatever equipment is available, since the production equipment will not be delivered until much later. In order to meet the plan for the start of production, the orders for manufacturing equipment will need to be placed sufficiently early to allow enough lead time for building, installing, and debugging. As shown in the illustration, the lead time requires that equipment orders be placed before the development of the process has been completed. And since the product design and the manufacturing process were developed independently, there is a reasonable chance that there will be a mismatch between the two. Since these problems will affect the design of the equipment, which has already been ordered, further redesign and process changes will be necessary after the equipment is delivered. Depending on how many iterations must be carried out in the design of the product, the process, and the equipment, the date for production will continue to slip.

Now let us look at the integrated approach represented in Figure 9-2(b). The design of the product and the manufac-

Figure 9-2. Investment decisions.

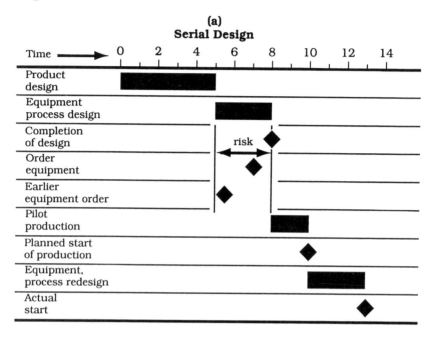

(a)
Serial Design

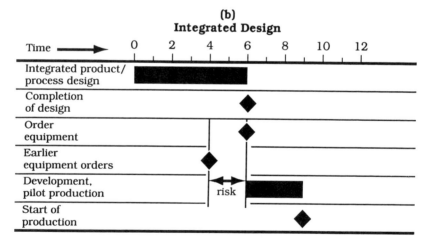

(b)
Integrated Design

turing process are carried out in a concurrent and integrated manner and are completed simultaneously—ideally, at the point where orders for manufacturing equipment must be placed to meet the lead time for building, installing, and debugging it. If the lead time of certain critical equipment is longer, risks of redesign will increase, depending on how long before design completion the orders must be placed.

Obviously, the ideal case involves having all the design and process finished before the equipment is ordered, so there is no risk at all. But this condition is impossible in any fast-moving, competitive business. In most cases, the development of critical production tools needed to advance product designs and processes also needs substantial lead times. Sometimes that lead time may be as long as the development of the product itself. The competence of the equipment suppliers and their relationship with the manufacturer play important roles in evaluating investment timing. These decisions will always entail significant risks, and companies must learn how to minimize them. The integrated process is clearly the better choice, because the experience and learning required to support these decisions are available much sooner. Furthermore, at any point in the design process, the integrated method will yield more knowledge than the serial system. This additional knowledge further reduces the risk if competitive pressures and other business conditions force an early decision to proceed with investments. And finally, the strength of the technical foundation for the design and process plays a major role in determining timing and risk involved in making these investment decisions.

How to Lower Your Risks

Your decisions on investment timing will depend on many technical and business factors. If you are in a competitive business, you may never have the luxury of making risk-free capital expenditures. But you can replace a wild gamble with a logical process of prudent steps that will justify the potential payoff. The key is the strength of the technical base and how rapidly and intelligently you carry out your product design, prototype, manufacturability, and manufacturing process program. The best way of making these capital investments is to complete as many of the early steps in the product development cycle as soon and as thoroughly as possible. This method is also the least costly in the long run.

Before making major capital investments, there are a series of questions that you can use as a guide to determine if and when you are ready:

1. What are the new and most important design features and manufacturing processes being incorporated into the product?

2. How confident are you that the technological foundation is strong enough to support these design and process advances?

3. What is the state of development of these advances, to what extent have they been proved, and what is the proof of their manufacturability? Are you confident that all these factors have reached a sufficiently advanced status to ensure that your equipment decisions are sound?

4. Are you attempting so many simultaneous and major advances that your investments are too risky, or are you confident that you are prudently controlling the number and magnitude of these advances?

5. If you plan to use outside suppliers to build the equipment, have you carefully checked their qualifications? What is your degree of confidence in them? Are they sufficiently integrated with your design and process development to ensure that the equipment they design and build will meet your requirements?

6. Have you tested the total product as a system? Have these tests been conducted with sufficient thoroughness so that you are satisfied that:

  • The system works?
  • The product design and the manufacturing processes will not demand major changes, which, in turn, would require that the equipment undergo significant redesign or even obsolescence?

7. Have you developed an architecture for your plant with a productive layout and work flow using the specifications of the equipment you are going to purchase? Do all the tools you plan to install fit into this architecture? Are you satisfied that the specifications for the equipment in speed, output, and reliability are based on realistic data?

It is no coincidence that many of these questions are similar to those asked in some of the previous chapters. The key steps on the critical path to building your foundation are the same as those that must be completed before you are ready to make investments in the production program. These questions require much more than simple yes or no answers. They necessitate extensive analysis of data; an intensive dialogue among many experts and many departments; a competent and experienced technical, production, and marketing team; and a strong and seasoned top management.

Once you have answered these questions, you will be in a much better position to determine the decisions you should make and the risks involved. If your answers to any *one* of these questions is negative, you may be taking an excessive risk. You will therefore need to reevaluate your program to determine the steps necessary to strengthen it. But if you can answer all these questions affirmatively, your program is sound. The time has come to make your investments and begin to move toward production.

Chapter 10

Learning: The Key to Shorter Product Cycles

We have now reviewed the overall concept of the product cycle and the six steps on the critical path that are essential to reduce its length. We know that the pace and success of a new product program depend on the priority and emphasis company management gives to these elements, the allocation of resources to perform them, and how they are integrated into a coherent management system. But as vital as these elements are, there is still a missing ingredient that is essential if a management system comprising all these elements is to work. That ingredient is the learning process and the corporate environment that makes that learning possible.

Organizational Learning

When we think of learning, we normally think of individuals acquiring skills or gaining information. A child learns to read, a production worker is trained to repair a machine, and a medical student is taught to perform surgical procedures. But learning is also a characteristic of groups and organizations. A new football team composed of experienced, professional players and a competent coach almost inevitably suffers through its first season in last place. But it eventually learns to perform its task as a team and moves up through the league standings, perhaps to become the champion. A newly formed orchestra, even with the best-trained professional musicians under the direction of a good conductor, lacks the cohesion and unity necessary to make great music, but time and experience playing together will gradually improve its performance. These athletic and musical organizations achieve this gradual improvement and eventual excellence through a collective learning process.

Like a football team and a symphony, a company developing a new product is also going through an extended period of learning, and the length of the product cycle is strongly influenced by the rate at which the total organization learns. The knowledge and experience gained at each step in the cycle—from research through product design, prototype testing, pilot production, manufacturing, and even into the customers' homes or offices—are part of the learning process. But that process will be slow unless management provides the right learning environment.

Organizations learn through a complex mosaic of individual skills and experiences, continual communication and dialogue, experimentation, trial and error, failure and success, and the knowledge that results from all of these. There are many personnel- and management-related issues that companies must address if this intricate process is to work. These issues directly influence how people function. Nobody can work well in an overheated and overcrowded room or in an atmosphere of constant anxiety about job security. Low employee morale, poor working conditions, and inadequate financial rewards can seriously reduce productivity, and they can have a profound effect on the rate of learning of both the individual and the entire company. These are obvious truths, and an enlightened management will do everything it can to prevent these conditions.

But there are other issues that influence the learning process and the length of the product cycle. Despite their importance, they are often given a low priority. These factors are:

- The degree of stability and continuity of the management chain
- The effectiveness of cross-functional teams
- The redundancy of levels in the management hierarchy
- The geographical proximity of the critical elements of the management system

All these factors are vital to the success of the product cycle and the learning process. Let us look at each of them to understand their importance.

Stability and Continuity in the Management Chain

Success in any job, whether it is shipping clerk or chairman of the board, depends on an extensive period of learning that includes acquisition of knowledge and extensive experience in performing the work. Even in the most menial task, knowledge is gained mostly by doing, not just by reading or listening. The more complex the job, the longer the period needed to learn how to do it.

Furthermore, organizations, like people, must learn. The effectiveness of an organization depends on how the individuals and groupings of people communicate and learn from one another, complement one another's skills, and work as a unit toward the achievement of a common goal. The longer they work together, the tighter their linkages and thought processes, the more they understand one another, and the more they collectively solve problems. Yet if the composition of the organization is constantly changing, the linkages break down and the learning process deteriorates. As a result, the organization actually *forgets,* necessitating a lengthy process of relearning.

Unfortunately, organizational instability is fostered by America's penchant for upward mobility; it is even aided and abetted by the companies themselves. Our management systems reward people handsomely for moving up through the management hierarchy. Usually, the fast movers are the most competent, aggressive, and motivated people in the work force. In a fast-growing company, such individuals rarely remain in a job for more than one or two years. They are constantly rising to higher positions of responsibility. Unfortunately, this constant movement can result in serious problems for both the employee and the company. These superstars never remain in a position long enough to develop professionalism, or a sense of ownership of a job. Their careers are built on the length of their curriculum vitae rather than sound accomplishment. They cannot be held accountable for results because they do not stay in one job long enough for their performance to be measured. While they move rapidly up the ladder, less talented and less aggressive employees remain stagnant in their positions. Consequently, the total organizational competence is reduced.

The instability created by constant movement in the management ranks can have serious ramifications for the product cycle. Learning is slower, accountability for performance is unclear, new communications links are continually forged and then broken, plans and strategies are constantly changing, and problems remain unsolved.

The defense establishment, in particular, is suffering from too much movement. In 1984, Congress passed a law requiring that managers of the military's multibillion-dollar acquisition programs stay on the job for at least forty-eight months. An article in *The New York Times* pointed out that despite this law, the tenure of program managers still averages less than two years, a fact that is creating instability, cost overruns, and technical problems in weapons programs.[1]

We can see how management instability influences the length of the product cycle by noting some of the roles of key managers:

- Make decisions on and plans for design and process approaches to meet certain program objectives; then obtain agreement on and support for these objectives from subordinates.
- Determine resources and capital required to carry out the plans.
- Obtain agreement and support from other organizations needed to implement these decisions.
- Win the confidence and trust of upper management.
- Sell decisions to upper management.

1. Eric Schmitt, "Quick Transfers in Arms Program Criticized," *The New York Times*, 2 July 1990.

- Build rapport with, win the confidence of, and maintain smooth communication channels with other departments.
- Give directions to carry out decisions.

Making these plans; creating a communications network; winning the confidence of employees, peers, and superiors; and getting the authority and support to do the job is a long process. But what happens if the manager is suddenly removed from that position? And what will the new manager do? Almost any new manager—anxious to place his or her own imprint on the new position, demonstrate rapid movement and results, and incorporate personal ideas about organizational direction, strategies, and management style— would move rapidly to make changes. The new manager would first take some time to study the program status, the roles and responsibilities of the major players, the skill capabilities and competence of subordinates, the power structure, and the communications channels and alliances that should be formed. But if the manager is aggressive, he or she is likely to move quickly and demonstrate authority by making substitutions in key positions or even making changes in tactics and strategy. In some cases, change may be called for, particularly if the previous management has failed. But in many instances, frequent changes only create and accelerate the process of organizational churning and instability.

Is this scenario unrealistic? It is not. In fact, many of these results of managerial change are inevitable, but it is easy to see how disruptive this type of change can be to the product cycle. And if there is too much movement too quickly, the consequences of the ensuing chaos could be disastrous. Between 1986 and 1992, IBM carried out four major reorganizations and sizable redistributions of personnel. We can only speculate whether these changes, made in attempts to solve problems, exacerbated IBM's difficulties and contributed to an acceleration of its recent misfortunes.

Of course, there is no way to completely eliminate change in the management chain. Incompetent managers must be removed, and vacancies in higher-level jobs must be filled with the best candidates. Some job rotation to give managers experience in others areas of the business can increase their versatility and breadth of experience; the Japanese have been successful in promoting this method of management training. And it is difficult to keep eager and ambitious stars in one position indefinitely. Furthermore, longevity can be a double-edged sword. Staying in one job too long can lead to parochialism, declining motivation, and ultimate burnout. Too much stability can also become a barrier to progress.

There is no simple rule to use to define the threshold point where stability turns into stagnation. Then what is the answer? Here are some guidelines a company can follow:

1. Make stability and continuity in the management chain a high priority.
2. Establish a goal of keeping the entire new product management team intact for the entire product cycle—from conception until manufacturing is well established.
3. Instead of rewarding management and other key people with early promotions, give them incentives to stay on the job until it is successfully completed.
4. Make movement to another position the exception, not the rule.
5. If a manager must be transferred from the program, replace him or her with a person who is already a part of the program, is highly knowledgeable about the plans, and has been a direct participant in making the program decisions. Such a replacement is less likely to reverse course and attempt to go in a new direction.

The Integrated Team

The importance of integrating the many interacting activities that take place in moving a product from invention to the customer has been a recurring theme of this book. This integration must take place by establishing very strong links between research, marketing, development, manufacturing, and purchasing. These bonds must be so tight that all of these departments must virtually function as one seamless whole.

The most commonly accepted method of achieving integration is through the use of interfunctional teams.

Teamwork can be defined as a cooperative effort by members of a group to achieve a common goal. But it is impossible to achieve a common goal if the members of the team keep changing. In order for a team to carry out its job successfully, team members must learn to communicate effectively by means of a common language; develop a strong rapport and mutual trust; learn the skills and capabilities of other members; and develop a comprehensive knowledge of the program and its history as it progresses. Decisions made at every step of the process must be understood, shared, and collectively applied. The ideas, knowledge, and insights of each team member are vital keys to problem solving and decision making. Achieving this strong working relationship requires a great deal of learning, and if the team composition changes too frequently, these intricate personal relationships will keep breaking down and the effectiveness of the team will deteriorate.

The team concept is potentially one of the most powerful means a company has to bring new ideas to the marketplace rapidly. But many companies are having difficulty using interdisciplinary teams effectively. The following problems are typical:

- Teams are created not as an organizational strategy to develop a product, but as a reaction to a crisis after serious problems have erupted.
- Team members are often inexperienced and thus are poor candidates to represent their respective functions. This often happens because management wants to keep its best people doing tasks it considers more important.
- The team is subject to the revolving-door syndrome, with membership constantly changing based on who management is willing to spare.
- Meetings are canceled because of the pressures created by the very problems the team has been formed to solve.
- Management ignores the recommendations of the team because it does not trust the judgment of the people it has put there.

Some of these problems occur because the technically skilled work force is too small and spread too thin. Management may sanction some of these practices because it gives only lip service and little support to the team concept. Often, department heads assign their weaker people to the team because they are afraid that a strong team will threaten their own power.

Many companies have difficulty establishing strong teams because the entrenched establishment resists the whole concept and there is no one to champion its cause. One company made considerable progress in instituting the use of teams because of the leadership of one executive who strongly believed in them. When he retired, however, there was nobody willing to continue to fight for the concept. As a result, teams were used with much less frequency, and their effectiveness deteriorated.

Lack of continuity of team membership is one of the most serious impediments to the use of teams as a means of achieving the integration that is essential to the management of the product cycle. Even the most casual follower of professional sports knows that a winning team requires continuity of its lineup for several years. Replacements should be made infrequently, and with only the most careful consideration of timing, quality, and fit with the team. One replacement in a string quartet, even a very competent one, can seriously degrade the quality of the performance; it may even spell the end of the partnership. These same characteristics of professional quality, compatibility, extensive training together, and a highly dedicated commitment to a common goal are essential to any company's program to create a new product and move it successfully to the marketplace.

There are a number of steps that management can take to make the team concept work:

1. Form the team at the very beginning of a project with a core membership that stays intact for the entire life of the program—until the product is successfully launched into manufacturing and the marketplace.
2. Staff the core of the team with the most competent and experienced people representing the areas that are es-

sential to the success of the product cycle and the solution of problems.

3. Give the team control of its destiny and the authority to do its job; insulate it from the constraints of bureaucracy.

4. Appoint a strong team leader who has the complete confidence of top management; then give the leader the authority and the resources to carry out his or her task.

5. At the beginning of the program, give the team members strong incentives to remain with the project throughout its duration and to achieve its objectives.

6. Evaluate and compensate individuals partially on the basis of the total team performance; motivate the members to work for the whole team's success.

7. Make long-term project-oriented teams a way of life and part of the company culture.

U.S. corporations are making some progress in implementing the team concept. In the Gemini survey of company executives (Appendix A), 40 percent of the respondents named integrated design teams as their first priority toward achieving shorter development cycles. All the companies described in the case studies in Appendix B are trying to institute teams.

Making teams work is not simple. Integrated teams are a radical departure from the ways of the past—in many ways circumventing and even removing power from the formal organizational structure. Only with the strongest leadership from the top will teams work, but they are an important means of expediting the learning process and shortening the product development cycle.

The Management Hierarchy

The next roadblock to corporate learning is a management chain overloaded with too many levels of management bureaucracy. In most U.S. corporations, large and small, there are simply too many people who can throw a wrench into the intricate machinery of the corporation. If the management structure becomes too complex, organizational gridlock can occur, seriously slowing down the pace of the learning process and lengthening the product development cycle.

Often, one or more layers of a management hierarchy are redundant, particularly in the middle-management ranks. The center of power and the capability to make policy and execute it exist in the upper executive levels, where responsibilities are clearly defined. The responsibilities of the lowest levels of management—the factory supervisor, the first-level engineering manager, or the local sales manager—are equally clear. They are directly on the firing line, the ones responsible for implementing policies, plans, and strategies by designing, manufacturing, and selling the products. They are also responsible for supervising some of the most important people in the company: the engineer in the laboratory, the worker on the factory floor, and the salesperson in the branch office. The management levels in between these two extremes often have no defined responsibilities, and their jobs are frustrating because they have no mission and little influence.

The plight of the middle manager is evident in the conduct of the product development cycle. Moving a new product through the process of design, development, and production entails countless decisions in policy, strategy, and detailed execution. A major part of the time used to accomplish this process is consumed in making these decisions. The more levels of management involved in this decision-making process, the longer it takes to carry it out. Middle managers are exactly that: stuck in the middle. They are not privy to vital information essential to the decision-making process, yet they cannot easily be ignored if the decisions involve their organizations. They must be informed and their opinions must be heard. If they do not support the proposed decisions, more time must be consumed trying to persuade them. All these layers of management inject a degree of inertia into the learning process far in excess of the value they contribute.

Companies attempt to deal with this top-heavy management bureaucracy in different ways. Many are "downsizing" their operations to reduce costs and increase productivity by massive reductions in their administrative and middle-management ranks. Apple Computer, IBM, Exxon, Control Data, Eastman Kodak, DuPont, and General Motors are examples of corporate giants that are moving aggressively in this direction.[2]

In order to accelerate the learning process, some companies bypass this managerial bureaucracy through an informal organization, as discussed in Chapter 3. Although there is a formal chart defining functions and responsibilities, an invisible but powerful network of alliances is formed independent of the formal hierarchy. These alliances are created by some of the strongest and most capable people who have worked together for long periods of time, have common professional interests, and share common goals. If the formal organization becomes a barrier to progress, these networks will actually circumvent them.

Economist John Kenneth Galbraith calls this informal power group the "technostructure." He claims that in most corporations, the power does not necessarily lie with the chairman, the president, or even the vice-presidential levels, but rather with the people who have the most information and knowledge. As an example, he cites the development of the atom bomb:

> In Los Alamos, during the development of the atomic bomb, Enrico Fermi rode a bicycle up the hill to work; Major General Leslie R. Groves presided in grandeur over the entire Manhattan District. Fermi had the final word on numerous questions of feasibility and design. In association with a handful of others, he could, at various early stages, have brought the entire enterprise to an end. No such power resided with Groves. At any moment he could have been replaced without loss and with possible benefit.[3]

2. Rod Willis, "What's Happening to America's Middle Managers?" *Management Review,* January 1987, pp. 24–33.

3. John Kenneth Galbraith, *The New Industrial State, 1st Edition* (Boston: Houghton Mifflin, 1967), p. 66. Copyright © 1967 by John Kenneth Galbraith. Reprinted by permission of Houghton Mifflin Co. All rights reserved.

Will either of these approaches—downsizing or informal networks—serve the long-term interests of industry in the management of the product cycle? The duplicate, informal organizational network is an expensive way to manage a company and hardly constitutes a long-term solution to low productivity and long development cycles. The "meat-axe" method of cutting the work force, in addition to ruining employee morale, may have short-term benefits but long-term risks unless the reductions are accomplished with great care and an effective new organizational structure replaces the old one.

The top-heavy management chain and the obsolete functional organizational structure are both serious barriers to the process of learning and to shorter development cycles. They must be gradually replaced by company decentralization and integration of the critical components of the product cycle through strong interdisciplinary teams. The transition will not be painless, but it is essential for any company in an industry in which competition is intense and technology is advancing.

Geography and Proximity for Good Communications

Continuity of management, fewer management levels, and integrated teams are important keys to providing the right organizational environment for learning. But their effectiveness is directly dependent on a fourth ingredient: a geographical environment that fosters good communication. But what is it, and how do we achieve it? Today, communication through the transmittal of information is very simple. Information technology; teleconferencing; express, voice, and electronic mail; satellite TV; facsimile; modem; and the cellular telephone make almost instantaneous communication at any time of day a simple matter. It certainly has made the transmission of astronomical volumes of data, production schedules, written reports, meeting times, and even the expected hour of arrival at home relatively straightforward. Without this technology of rapid communication, modern-day business would be impossible to conduct. But today, the traditional meaning of communication has changed dramatically. Transmission of information and data, no matter how fast or voluminous, is simply not enough.

Practically every recent book on the subject of competitiveness, including this one, emphasizes the importance of revamping the modern-day corporate organization. Barriers must be broken down, independent functions must be integrated, new measurement systems must be installed, and jobs must be restructured. Engineers, production managers, marketing specialists, controllers, and even researchers must be in constant contact with one another. For example, one of the most critical parts of the entire product development process (see Chapter 6) is the design of the product for manufacturability and quality. No other part of the entire spectrum of activities carried on in a corporation requires more day-by-day, even hour-by-hour contact between scientists, designers, purchasing agents, manufacturing engineers, and even factory workers. In order to carry out these contacts, they need to go well beyond communication. They need to conduct a continuing dialogue which far exceeds mere communication. A dialogue is a conversation between two people, with an exchange of ideas or opinions. The development process involves a constant exchange of ideas between people whose expertise and ideas must contribute to it. Yet even dialogue is not enough— there must be synergism.

Synergism is the interaction of two or more agents to achieve a total effect that is greater than the sum of the individual effects. We have all experienced it. How often have we witnessed the following phenomenon? Two or more people, each with a proposal for solving a problem, meet to exchange their ideas. After they have shared, discussed, and reflected on all the ideas, each begins to modify his or her proposal based on the influence of the others. Eventually, the group agrees on a solution that consists of elements of each original idea. The solution is more powerful than any of those proposed by the individual participants—the whole is greater than the sum of its parts. In fact, some of the participants may not even recognize their specific contributions to the solution, even though they were vital to the process of developing it.

Designing a product that is reliable and manufacturable,

defining a market for a new product, developing a corporate plan that will work, mapping out a long-range corporate strategy, and developing a new technology all require constant and extensive dialogue and synergy. Yet none of this can be accomplished without an additional dimension—physical proximity.

Out of Sight, Out of Mind

Remember the old college or army friends from whom you were absolutely inseparable? Your entire lives were tightly linked on the battlefield, in class, at the canteen, or at football games and parties. You shared the same experiences and understood what made the other tick. Then you returned to civilian life or graduated from college and went your separate ways, usually to different cities or states. Remember what happened twenty years later when you attended a reunion of the graduating class or the army division? You were reunited with your old buddies; you exchanged excited slaps on the back, much camaraderie, and reminiscences of the good old days. But ten minutes later, the euphoria had run its course, and you had little more to say. You were strangers, leading separate lives, having had totally different experiences. The bonds that had held you together had not only loosened, they were completely untied. The continuity of the day-to-day association had been broken, distance had separated you, and you had become strangers. You were out of sight and out of mind.

In the world of business, this type of scenario is repeated again and again. People who work in the same physical location, are motivated by the same goals, and are rewarded for success in achieving the same objectives form the same tight links as army or college friends. But when those links are cut, and when people move on to other jobs at other locations, the bonds formed by close proximity, continuity, and common interests quickly dissolve.

A great deal of communication can be achieved by modern-day technology regardless of the distance between the communicators, but the most critical interactions cannot. A continuing and meaningful dialogue between people work-

ing toward a common goal must be conducted in close proximity. This dialogue and the synergy arising from it cannot
occur with only an occasional meeting or telephone call. The
people working together must develop close bonds. They must
interact continuously. They must develop a sense of fraternity
and common purpose. Like the army buddies, they must be
fighting in the same foxhole together every day, not meeting
once a month in a conference room remote from each other's
work location. The Bell Telephone Laboratories and the Western Electric Company recognized this fact by geographically
dispersing some of their applied research to the Western Electric manufacturing plants over forty years ago (see Chapter 5).[4]

The Perils of Geographical Dispersal

The penalty for the geographical separation of people
working on the same project can be severe. The Acme Corporation, a real company with a disguised name, manufactured
automobile parts. It designed its products in a laboratory situated approximately a mile from its primary manufacturing
plant. Four other plants that made the same product were
located in remote locations ranging from 500 to 2,000 miles
away. Acme introduced a continual line of new products into
its five plants almost simultaneously. Unfortunately, there
were serious manufacturability and quality problems on almost every new product. After the products were delivered to
the marketplace, customer complaints revealed flaws in dimensional tolerances, performance, packaging, and labeling.
The volume of engineering changes required to solve these
problems cascaded into a torrent. Simple problems that could
have been anticipated, prevented, or solved much earlier by a
close dialogue between the designer and the manufacturer
were now being discovered too late to prevent cost increases
and a loss of reputation with customers.

There were plenty of excuses for this state of affairs. Management discouraged design engineers from traveling to the
remote manufacturing locations because of the cost. The de-

4. J. A. Morton, *Organizing for Innovation* (New York: McGraw-Hill,
1971).

sign engineers were strangers to the people at these plants, and it was difficult to institute a meaningful and productive dialogue. Communication between the engineers and the staff at the manufacturing plant only one mile away was only slightly better. Even this short distance and the fact that the design and manufacturing activities were in different buildings were sufficient barriers to communication. Distance, even a short one, created a wall that reinforced the insular, compartmentalized, and even adversarial nature of the relationships between the engineering and manufacturing groups.

Very small companies do not have this problem. The cottage industries of Italy are good examples. Throughout the country, invisible to the outside world and possibly even to the tax collector, is an almost endless chain of these small family businesses. They have no problems with bureaucracy, staffs, or communication across building, city, or state boundaries. They are highly productive enterprises that capitalize on their skills unencumbered by the type of problems discussed in this book. But most U.S. companies do not have the luxury of operating out of the family basement or garage. There is no practical way to house a large company in one room, one building, and, in some cases, maybe not even one state or country. Furthermore, there are many valid reasons for companies to have multiple locations. They may do so to improve distribution of their products, utilize labor skills in different areas of the country or abroad, limit the size of their employee populations in a given area, or establish a presence in other states or in foreign countries to increase their markets.

Clearly, geographical separation of the organizations participating in the invention, design, development, and launch of a new product or technology can be a serious impediment to the product cycle. But companies can minimize these barriers by:

- Treating the issue of geographical proximity of the critical parts of the product cycle as a high priority in planning or rearranging space and new buildings.
- Housing the entire integrated design team, including the product designers, manufacturing engineers, prototype builders, purchasing personnel, and research

support, at the manufacturing location. Place them as close together as possible, with particular emphasis on the proximity of the design and manufacturing engineers.

• Introducing a product that will be manufactured at several locations at the plant that contains the team first, then dispersing it to other locations when the manufacturing process is under control.

Stability, team integration, a tight management hierarchy, and geographical proximity are all vital to the company learning process and the effective management of the product cycle. In Japanese industry, these practices are characteristics of the company and country culture. In many ways, these important elements run against the grain of U.S. industrial and national behavior. But they are essential, and many of America's best corporations are beginning to take steps in this direction.

Chapter 11

Managing the Critical Path

So far we have explored the key elements of the critical path to the shortened product cycle as well as certain environmental policies and practices that directly influence it. But to make the story complete, there is one additional ingredient that is essential to achieving competitiveness through shorter product cycles. That component is the role of top management in the direction of the cycle itself. The highest echelons of the company, including the chief executive officer (CEO), must be major, direct participants in the execution of the management system that brings the new product from concept to marketplace. If top management is remote and detached, the system will not work.

In the past, a company's technical and production arms have not usually been considered the direct responsibility of top management. Corporate executives in most U.S. corporations have been primarily preoccupied with finance and sales, delegating the management of the product cycle to more specialized and experienced subordinates. At the time, the detachment of top management from this part of the management process worked, largely due to the nature of technology and because there was much less pressure from foreign competitors for higher quality, lower cost, and shorter time to market. The organizational compartments could operate somewhat independently, and the corporate office presiding over them could measure their performance individually. If the sales figures were low, the CEO could blame the sales department; if the costs were too high, he could hold the plant manager accountable; if the product did not meet performance or reliability specifications, he could, in most cases, attribute the problem to poor product design. But today, this type of management will not work. Advancing technology, product complexity, and the need for greater company integration have made the deep involvement of top management a necessity.

Involving Top Management in the Product Cycle

Among the most frequently cited reasons for our lack of competitiveness are the short-term vision of American executives and their lack of involvement in managing the introduction of new products. In some respects, this perception of detachment is not entirely correct. Top management often becomes deeply involved, but unfortunately in the wrong places. One form of such direct intervention is the "micromanagement" of serious production crises and outbreaks of customer dissatisfaction. Until these problems occur, the top echelons of the company are usually remote from the product cycle. But when they do occur, top management is catalyzed into action, bypassing lower management layers in an attempt to fix the problems itself. However, masterminding the details of the product cycle or second-guessing the engineers or manufacturing managers is definitely not top management's job and, except in rare circumstances, it is neither qualified nor in a position to do so. Of course, crisis management is difficult to resist, and there are even times when this type of intervention is essential, but as a long-term management style, it is dangerous. It will not enhance competitiveness or shorten the product cycle because it does not attack any of the fundamental problems.

There is another form of executive interaction that is essential to a corporation's ability to compete through the more rapid introduction of new products and technologies. That involvement entails a much closer association with the overall direction of the product cycle and taking a leadership role in it. Yet in most U.S. corporations, the top executives do not play that role, even though they are the only ones with the position and power to do so. Practically every one of the key elements of the cycle that we have explained in this book demands the involvement of top management.

Of course, most of the activity involved in the product cycle is carried out in the laboratories, on the factory floor, at the supplier, and in the interdisciplinary teams that are formed to create the linkages between all these activities. If the program management and the technical and manufacturing capability of these areas are strong, most of the work required to design, develop, and manufacture the product should be accomplished with little intervention from the top. But although top executives should not become embroiled in these details, they must be involved in several high-level issues that are vital to the conduct of the product cycle. These responsibilities can be divided into five categories:

1. Setting the strategies and making the investment decisions
2. Integrating the business
3. Creating the right learning environment
4. Institutionalizing the system
5. Assessing the performance of the total management system

Now let us look at why top management must become involved in each of these issues.

Strategies and Investment Decisions

Three types of decisions must be made at the top, or at least near the top—at the level of the head of an autonomous business unit. Each relates to one or more of the six critical elements we have discussed:

1. *New product strategy (Chapter 4).* The formulation of new product strategy involves practically every part of the corporation, including research, engineering, marketing, manufacturing, planning, finance, and personnel. No other decision has such far-reaching im-

plications for the revenue, profit, growth, and competitiveness of a company.

2. *Resource allocation.* Top management must approve
   the plans for allocating sufficient money and personnel to carry out the major parts of the product cycle,
   including applied research, integrated product design,
   and prototype testing (Chapters 5, 6, and 7).

3. *Investments.* Top management must approve the ex-
   penditure of major capital investments to build the
   factory and order the production tools for large-scale
   manufacturing (Chapter 9).

Who is involved in making these decisions? Teams of
marketing specialists, scientists, design and process engineers, plant supervisors, and purchasing agents participate in
assembling the data and developing the details of these strategies, plans, and investment proposals. Several levels of
management participate in formulating the final recommendations. But only the top executives can be the final arbiters.
They are the only ones who have responsibility for directing
all the organizational units involved in these decisions, the
only ones who can set priorities and allocate funds and are
accountable to the customers and the stockholders for the
company's performance. Furthermore, they must reconcile
the needs of each program with all the other demands for resources, the cost of the products currently in the marketplace,
and the profit objectives of the company. And the consequences of a bad decision can be very serious. Millions of dollars, market share, the price of company stock, and
competitive position in the industry may all be at stake. If
senior company executives abdicate their responsibilities in
these areas, they leave a tremendous vacuum.

Integration

Corporate integration can be achieved only through major change. Only the top executives of the company have the
necessary authority to implement it and make it work. The
organizational realignments and cross-functional teams necessary to form the critical linkages between the parties that

drive the major elements of the product cycle require new skills, relationships, human behavior, and management roles and responsibilities. They mark significant departures from the way companies have operated in the past, and these major changes will take place only with aid and impetus from the top.

The Right Learning Environment

Chapter 10 discussed certain geographical, organizational, and behavioral characteristics that are essential to the acceleration of the learning process and a shorter product development cycle. Each of these characteristics, including job continuity, geographical proximity, and fewer levels of organizational hierarchy, entails significant new directions. They involve new management practices, personnel policies, methods of measurement and reward, and priorities for the planning, construction, and allocation of space. Only the power and authority of top management can make these changes happen.

The Product Development Management System: Personalization vs. Institutionalization

Every organization in a company bears the imprint of its leader, whether it be a supervisor of a production line, a manager of a department, or the chief executive. That leader establishes policies, sets priorities, and determines the style of the operation. Each new leader attempts to place his or her own imprint on the organization, make changes, chart new directions, and set a different tone. It is not uncommon for a department's organizational structure to be revamped every time a new manager takes over. Consequently, a major problem companies face in instituting change is trying to make it stick. Instead of having stable, institutionalized practices and structures, organizations are often built around personalities. One strong individual with dedication and commitment to a particular course of action can make it happen, but once that person leaves, the change disappears. For example, one executive of a midwestern corporation was a strong proponent of integrated product and process design. After a great deal of struggle and despite strong opposition from entrenched traditional engineering and manufacturing management, he succeeded in implementing it. But soon after he began to make progress he retired. Many of the practices he pioneered began to evaporate, and the organization reverted to its former state. So unless higher management is also deeply committed to perpetuating these changes and is willing to do what is necessary to retain them, a reversion to old habits is almost inevitable.

The Management System's Performance

One of the greatest difficulties top executives face is how to measure performance, diagnose problems, and take action. Certain data such as the number of products produced and shipped, sales demand, overall profit and loss, and total corporate revenues are essential, and they are relatively simple to assemble and understand. But these measurements have their limitations. They inform management how good or bad things are, but they do not tell it why or what to do next. It is this lack of insight into the performance of the infrastructure of the corporation and how it is really working that is changing the role of management and forcing a greater degree of management involvement in the product cycle.

In the past, when companies could operate effectively with nonintegrated engineering, marketing, and manufacturing functions, top management could measure the overall performance of each of these groups individually. But in this era of highly complex technology, it is increasingly difficult to identify and distinguish between individual and departmental responsibilities, which in turn complicates the tasks of measuring performance, rewarding success, identifying the source of problems, and taking corrective action. Because of the blurring of the lines of demarcation between elements of the product cycle, it is no longer easy to point the finger of responsibility at any single individual or group.

Some examples can be found in Chapter 5, which discusses three problems that occurred in the course of new product programs because of unanticipated and previously undetected defects. These defects could have arisen from any one of a number of sources. For example, was the IBM System 360 reliability problem due to metallurgical failure during the production scale-up period? Was this defect due to poor product design? Could it have resulted from inadequate fundamental understanding of complex metallurgical systems? Did the manufacturing organization pay inadequate attention to the scale-up characteristics of production tools? Did marketing seriously underestimate the market? Or was the problem caused by poor management judgment concerning the feasibility of the planned production buildup? In fact, it could have been caused by any one or even all of these factors. This example illustrates the challenge in identifying errors, determining the causes, and finding the solutions. It also demonstrates the need for new management roles, organizational structures, and measurement methods that are consistent with these new characteristics of modern-day technology.

Are U.S. Executives Capable of Managing the Product Development Cycle?

If U.S. managers must play a more direct role in the orchestration of the product cycle, are they capable of doing it? There are two questions concerning the ability of top U.S. executives to manage technology-driven companies in this era of fierce worldwide competition: Do they have the technical skills, and are they sufficiently focused on the long-term plans of their businesses? In many companies, the answer to both questions is no, but with some effort on the part of the executives themselves, the answers can become yes.

Do they have the right technical skills? Must they be engineers or scientists? Many of Japan's most successful companies are led by technically trained executives. David Packard of Hewlett-Packard and Robert Noyce of Intel were highly skilled engineers who managed their companies to positions of leadership in their fields. Yet James Houghton, chairman of the highly successful Corning, majored in history; Thomas J. Watson, Jr., who led IBM to a commanding leadership position in the computer industry during the 1950s and 1960s, had little technical training and began his career as a salesman. There are many dimensions to an effective leader of a technologically advanced company; technical skill is only one of them. A strong technical background is a definite advantage, but an engineer without leadership and management capability can fail, and a political science major with these abilities can succeed.

Are they sufficiently oriented toward the long term? A widespread belief exists that Americans' penchant for quick profits, brought about by our tax system and stockholder avarice, drives corporate management's short-term vision. This short-term psychology was cited by the academics and executives polled in the Gemini studies (see Appendix A) as a serious problem facing U.S. industry today. But even if this problem were to suddenly disappear—a most welcome but unlikely event—it is debatable whether a sudden shift in management's behavior would occur. However, there are steps that top executives can take to expand their field of vision and play a major part in the development of new products, including:

1. Studying to acquire enough knowledge about products and technologies to communicate with subordinates and make intelligent decisions. A Ph.D. in physics is not a prerequisite; many astute executives without technical training have learned enough about the technical aspects of their business to supplement their management skills and become effective leaders.

2. Placing their most trusted, technically competent, and experienced people with strong knowledge of the industry and its products in those key management positions that are critical to the product development cycle.

3. Leading a top management team made up of these key people, developing a close working relationship with them, and listening to their advice.

4. Using this team's assistance in making the major strategic, planning, and investment decisions that are essential to the success of the product cycle and in monitoring progress, identifying problems, and finding solutions.

5. Devoting only a small amount of time, perhaps only 5 to 10 percent, to studying detailed day-to-day sales and production statistics, and resisting the temptation to bypass the management team and attempt to solve short-term problems alone. Subordinates should be able to handle these problems, and if they cannot, they should be replaced.

Even with the highest resolve, corporate management will have a great deal of difficulty changing its current mode of operation. Making the transition from tactical, short-term firefighting to long-term strategy and corporate growth will be difficult. But the only center of corporate power capable of creating lasting change is at the highest executive level, and depending on the structure of the company, that may even mean the chief executive office. Only these top executives have the authority and stature to insist and ensure that these changes are built into the fabric of the corporate organization, management process, and company culture. Their involvement is a key factor in shortening the product cycle and making it work.

Chapter 12

Epilogue

The only way to establish a lasting solution to any serious problem is to find its fundamental cause and remove it. I believe that the integrated application of the technical, operational, and behavioral factors that form the critical path I have discussed in this book, if applied with the right emphasis and timing, attacks these fundamental issues and treats the basic reasons for high costs, poor quality, excessively long product cycles, and our lagging technological growth.

These critical elements of the product cycle are the ingredients that can provide U.S. manufacturers with the margin of superiority in quality, product advancement, and speed to market that is essential to achieve industry leadership. Each of these elements is highly dependent on the others. All must be managed as an intricate mosaic of highly integrated components in which many of the roles and relationships are rewritten and the old organizational lines of demarcation disappear. That is why top management must drive the necessary changes within the corporation and must be deeply involved in making this integrated organizational process work effectively.

What is new about the message in this book? I have emphasized several key areas that have been given far too little attention by U.S. industry. Yet it is precisely these components that are the most important. In order to accelerate the pace of technological advance and get to the marketplace faster with new and innovative products that the customer wants, U.S. companies must:

1. Carefully choose the level of technological change they attempt and the degree of risk they can afford.

2. Build a sound technical basis for their products with the greatest emphasis on those critical areas that require a strong technical and scientific foundation.

3. Tightly integrate the design of the product, the manufacturing process, and the manufacturing plant.

4. Integrate the total product as a complete system using simulation and physical prototypes, then rigorously analyze and test it to identify and remove deeply embedded, incipient defects in design, process, product performance, and reliability.

5. Take all these steps before making major investment decisions.

6. Institutionalize practices that promote rapid learning through organizational stability, job continuity, and physical proximity.

7. Ensure that the supplier of critical components takes these same steps and is an integral partner in the design of the total product.

There is one more important factor that must be considered: Every company in a competitive industry is racing to keep pace with rapid technological change and products of increasing complexity. Because of this continual advancement, corporations must operate in a dynamic state of constant learning. In this environment, the pursuit of new knowledge and experience is perpetual, the outcome is always unpredictable, and risk is always present. The reality is that U.S. industry is equipped to cope with stability, not change. The outmoded, functional organization with its emphasis on the bottom line and incremental cost improvements worked in a time when technology was static and foreign competition weak. That era is gone, and a much more demanding one has arrived. The challenge to management is to learn how to master this environment of learning, uncertainty, and risk.

Why will these steps lead U.S. companies to their goal of shorter cycles, better products, and greater market share? Because:

- Solutions to inevitable problems are fundamental and permanent instead of being temporary, expensive, and ineffective Band-Aids.

- Mistakes are discovered and corrected early when they are less costly instead of too late when the price in time, quality, and customer satisfaction is too high.
- Critical parts of the development process that are highly interrelated are carried out simultaneously and integratively instead of sequentially and independently.
- The complex process of learning is greatly accelerated because it is carried out in an organizational and human environment that promotes it.

And what is most important of all, it creates the long-range conditions that will form the basis for a rapidly and continuously advancing stream of new products that will meet the demands of consumers throughout the world.

The health of the American economy is directly related to our ability to compete in global markets. And the growth of our industrial base is the key to reducing our enormous trade and federal deficits, generating capital for further industrial expansion, revitalizing our infrastructure, rebuilding our cities, revamping our environmental system, and solving some of our most pressing social problems. It would be highly presumptuous to claim that shortening the product cycle will achieve all these monumental objectives. But moving products to market by accelerating the pace of advancement of technology is certainly an important ingredient in the solution to our economic woes. It may well be the most important means of regaining our industrial momentum and international leadership.

Much of the discussion in this book revolves around the roles of the researchers, engineers, and managers as major participants in the product cycle. Conspicuously absent is a discussion of the role of the manufacturing workers, the people most closely associated with the actual production of the final product, and certainly one of the most important groups of employees of any industrial enterprise. So why have I left them out? Media coverage of the subject of productivity and competitiveness keeps referring to the fact that the productivity of the American worker has not increased fast enough and lags behind that of our foreign competitors. This assertion conjures up visions of unmotivated employees just going through the motions on the production line or wasting time at the water fountain. I believe that nothing could be farther from the truth. The American worker on the factory floor is undoubtedly as capable, dedicated, and motivated as his or her counterparts in other parts of the world. It is not the worker on the assembly line who is contributing to our lagging productivity or long development cycles. By the time the product reaches the production floor, it has already encountered the most serious delays in the program. In addition, it is the entire product development management system that fails to provide the worker with the designs, tools, and training necessary for competitive manufacturing.

What are the prospects for the future? Can industry take bold steps to institute the reforms that are essential to manage the critical path to shorter development cycles in an era of increasing technological demands? When I began this book, I was concerned that some of my proposals were too difficult to implement in the current U.S. industrial and economic environment. I was also somewhat pessimistic about the state of U.S. manufacturing and our ability to turn it around. Reading the material that has been written on this subject and interviewing academic leaders who were studying it in depth only supported my negative outlook.

On careful reflection, however, perhaps I have been overly pessimistic. I have not yet been converted from a bear to a charging bull, but I believe that there are some positive signs of change in U.S. industry. I do not claim that my ideas are revolutionary in concept; no one is likely to quarrel with them. Many recent books, including those listed in the Bibliography, have treated different aspects of this subject. All these works contribute to the new consciousness of this problem and some of the approaches to its solution. But I have added several new issues that have not been discussed as keys to the product cycle and have put more emphasis on and given a different interpretation to the meaning of others.

Many of the executives I interviewed are attempting to take some of the measures I recommend. Although they recognize the difficulties in implementing these steps and agree that it may be too early to fully assess their effect, they are confident that they are going in the right direction. Of course, these companies represent a very small sample of the thousands of industrial corporations in the United States. Nevertheless, they do include some of our most progressive organizations, and it is hoped that they will demonstrate within the next few years that these actions will pay off in the arena of international competitiveness.

Regaining our worldwide industrial leadership will take an enormous effort, a strong dedication to change, patience, and time to bring it about. There are no simple and inexpensive shortcuts. But the path I have proposed will be worth the price, and it will lead to success.

Appendix A

U.S. Industry and Competition: How Good—or Bad—Are We?

There is a constant drumbeat of alarms sounded in books, the press, and television concerning the alleged decline in the competitive position of U.S. industry, the migration of many of our industries abroad, the invasion of foreign capital and management to run our manufacturing plants, our massive trade deficit, and our productivity stagnation. An article in the June 1989 *Scientific American* discussing the findings of the MIT Commission on Industrial Productivity states that

> American industry has also been handicapped by shrinking time horizons and a growing preoccupation with short-term profits. There have been many recent instances in which U.S. firms have lost market share to overseas competitors despite an early lead in technology, sales, or both. Often these firms effectively cede a potential market by not "sticking to their knitting." Instead, they diversify into activities that are more profitable in the short run.[1]

1. Suzanne Berger, Michael L. Dertouzos, Richard M. Lester, Robert M. Solow, and Lester C. Thurow, "Toward a New Industrial America," *Scientific American,* June 1989, pp. 34–47.

In somewhat more colorful language, Richard Darman, President Bush's budget director, attributes our competitive problems to the claim that

> we consume today as if there were no tomorrow. We attend too little to the issues of investment necessary to make tomorrow brighter. Like the spoiled 50's child in the recently revived commercial, we seem on the verge of a collective now-now scream: "I want my Maypo, I want it nowwww!"

Authors of books on this subject, like everyone else, have their own opinions, and by now you have probably discovered mine. Before setting out to write this book, and in order to avoid being too heavily influenced by my own prejudices as well as by this chorus of gloom, I, in collaboration with colleagues from Gemini Consulting, set out to determine how others involved in the U.S. industrial scene perceived our competitive problems and what we should be doing to solve them. By comparing the views of these people we hoped to gain some perspective on the subject of how well—or poorly—U.S. industry was doing. Perhaps they would have different opinions, or at least express some ideas that could lead to potential solutions. First, we personally interviewed twenty-one professors from many of the most prestigious graduate schools of business and engineering, people who are authorities on competitiveness and who have published widely on the subject. These academics are continually feeling the pulse of industry through research, case studies, and constant contacts with executives. Next, in cooperation with the American Management Association, we surveyed a cross section of approximately 200 senior executives who are directly involved in manufacturing in a wide range of industries. We used a comprehensive questionnaire as a guide for the interviews and surveys. Although the questions differed somewhat for the two groups, there was enough overlap in them to determine any common or diverging themes. The results were thought-provoking, and I summarize them here.

The View From Academia

In assessing the state of U.S. industrial competitiveness, all but one professor, who did not venture an opinion, stated that with few exceptions, U.S. industry is not only trailing, but losing ground or barely keeping pace with our foreign competitors (Figure A-1). A few expressed the opinion that in certain industries such as housing, food processing, aircraft, and possibly chemicals and pharmaceuticals, the picture is not quite as bleak, primarily because there is less competitive pressure. One participant observed that "we have had a myopic, unrealistic view of manufacturing based on unrealistic expectations," since we were leaders only when we had no competition. Another academic compared our industrial problem to that of Britain twenty years ago.

Next, we asked them what societal and governmental problems external to companies act as barriers to competitiveness (Figure A-2). All of us get a daily dose of media coverage citing a deficient educational system, restrictive tax structure, and unfair trade practices of our foreign competitors as the primary culprits contributing to our competitive difficulties. To some extent, the academics we interviewed echoed some of these opinions. Over half cited the quality of our secondary educational system as being a serious handicap. The remainder listed cost of capital, tax policies, and the lack of long-term investment incentives. Some of their comments included observations that "social degeneration and greed," excessively high executive pay, and a deemphasis on

Figure A-1. Where U.S. industry stands.

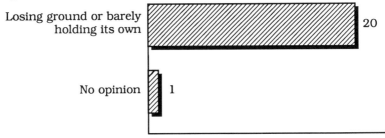

Losing ground or barely holding its own — 20

No opinion — 1

Figure A-2. Primary external factors.

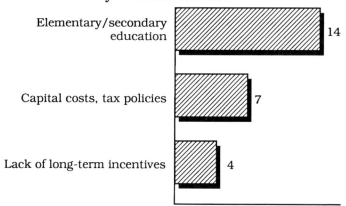

quality in a consumer-driven economy all played a part. One interviewee observed that our problems are not related to the political or legislative environment per se, but rather to "uncertainty" created by constant changes in this environment that make it difficult for companies to compete.

Yet despite all these discouraging observations, two-thirds of the academics expressed the surprising view that these external factors were *not* the principal reasons for our competitive difficulties. They believe that if a magic wand suddenly made these environmental factors evaporate, our difficulties in competing would not disappear. The reason: Problems that are *internal* to companies are much more serious (Figure A-3).

What are the problems to which they refer? Most attributed our declining competitiveness to weaknesses in manufacturing and the role it plays in the corporation. Specifically, they believe that manufacturing is not integrated with the rest of the company, and it is not used as a strategic weapon in the company arsenal. Most of the remainder of the academics expressed the opinion that management of U.S. corporations operates with too short-range a view, preventing it from making the investments in research, development, and production capability necessary to develop new products and technologies.

The next question related to the value of technology prac-

Figure A-3. Primary internal company factors.

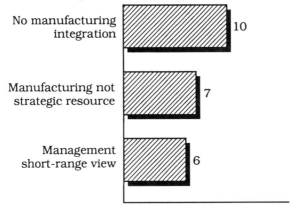

tices and tools such as Computer Aided Design and Computer Aided Manufacturing (CAD/CAM), Computer Integrated Manufacturing (CIM), Materials Requirements Planning (MRP), design-for-assembly methods, statistical process control, and automation. These are the tools that have been widely publicized as solutions to our competitive problems. Surprisingly, the interviewees *unanimously* expressed the strong conviction that these tools have not been very effective, that they have been oversold, misapplied, and poorly implemented (Figure A-4). Furthermore, when asked to comment on U.S. industry's use of such highly touted Japanese practices as Just-In-Time and Kanban, three-quarters of the respondents believed that they had also been misapplied with little payoff, and the remainder believed that they had achieved limited success in some industries. These professors did not claim that these practices and tools would never work. They did believe, however, that in the current environment,

Figure A-4. The value of technologies.

considering the way most companies operate today, these methods have not been used effectively. In order to capitalize on the potential of these methods, changes in the manner in which companies operate are mandatory. One academic, echoing the consensus of the group, asserted that "these are management, not technical failures."

If these Japanese practices and widely advertised technology tools have not met our expectations, and if these professors are correct in their view that the primary barriers to competitiveness are within, not outside, the corporation, what must change within companies? In answer to this question, the academics expressed a strong belief that our corporations were too fragmented and compartmentalized, and that manufacturing, in particular, played a subservient and detached role in the company. Consequently, they expressed strong opinions that major changes should involve company organization and priorities, stressing the need for strengthening the role of manufacturing and integrating it more closely with the corporate strategy and the product design process.

Can U.S. management face up to these needs and make these changes? The academic leaders were not very optimistic. The consensus among them was that although U.S. corporations have the capability to change, they probably will not because corporate management has neither the will, the motivation, nor the sense of urgency to make changes. Many stated that it would take a unique form of corporate leadership to bring about the reforms that are necessary to put U.S. industry back on the competitive track (see Figure A-5).

Can American society change? Do we have the capability to adopt the necessary improvements in our educational system or revisions in our tax and economic policies to stimulate growth and promote a longer-range focus by company management? Again, these academics were not very optimistic (Figure A-6). One articulated what most of them believed: that ours is a "Pearl Harbor" society, requiring some type of cataclysmic event to force change.

Will the trend of globalization of corporations help us? Although half the academics believed that we could profit from it, they were pessimistic about our ability to capitalize

Figure A-5. Keys to regaining competitiveness.

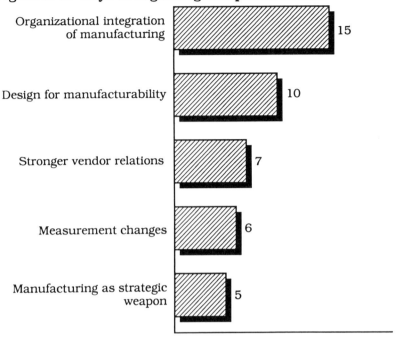

Figure A-6. America's resolve to change.

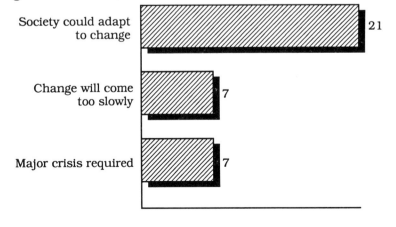

Figure A-7. Impact of globalization.

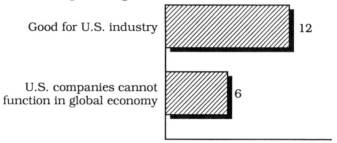

on its advantages, primarily due to our lack of knowledge of foreign languages and cultures (Figure A-7). One participant observed that the American "executive's field of view stops at Martha's Vineyard and Catalina Island."

We asked the group how they felt about the current trend of foreign investment in U.S.-based manufacturing such as Honda, Phillips, and Thompson. Most of them believed that this trend will help U.S. industry because we will learn much from their management practices (Figure A-8). Some believed that foreign management of our companies and the lessons we will learn from it will actually save us!

This perspective from academia is not very reassuring. These representatives of our leading graduate schools were clearly very pessimistic about our current competitive state in the world. Are they right? Are things really that bad? Let us now turn to the opinions of the executives.

Figure A-8. Impact of foreign companies' investment and management on U.S. companies.

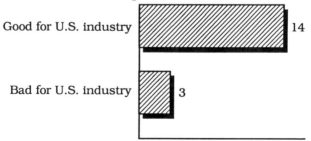

The View From the Executive Suite

We surveyed 200 executives, including CEOs and vice-presidents of manufacturing and operations from a wide range of companies in many industries (Figure A-9). This group represents the company managers directly on the firing line, who know intimately how their companies are performing and have a good understanding of their competition, their products, and the marketplace. We asked them to give us their views on a number of issues relating to the performance of their own companies and how well they were doing relative to their competition.

First, we asked them how competitive they are in their own industries as well as the prospects for the future. Almost two-thirds of the respondents claimed that their respective companies are leaders or near the top of their industries in market share, although slightly less said that they are leading or near the top with respect to profits (Figure A-10). In addition, approximately half believed that their companies are showing an increasing trend in market share; most of the remainder thought that their portions of the market were static. They viewed the future for their profits less optimistically. Less than half believed that their trends in profits were continuing upward. Although these numbers were not very

Figure A-9. Company and executive profile.

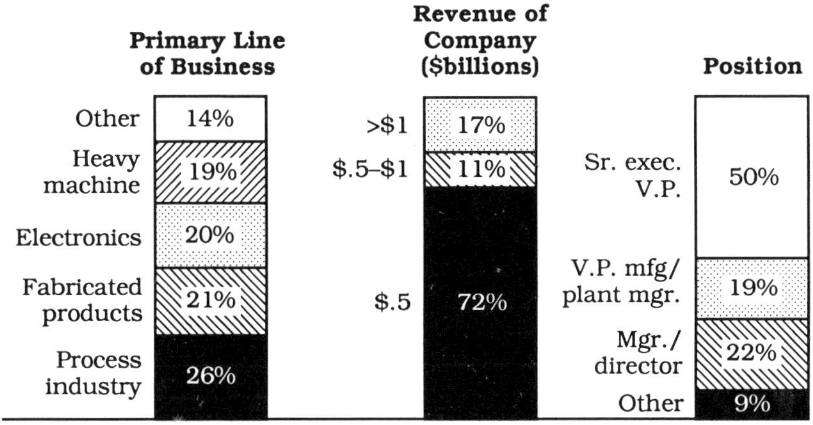

Figure A-10. Executives' view of their companies.

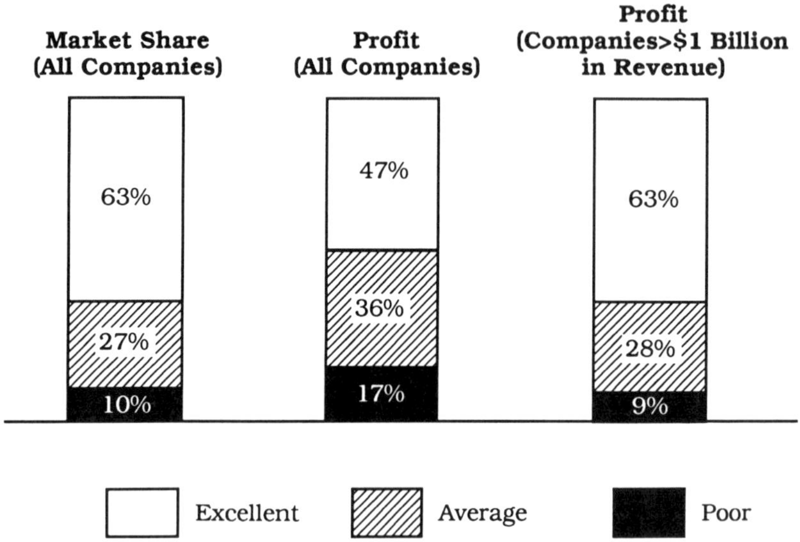

Market Share (All Companies)	Profit (All Companies)	Profit (Companies>$1 Billion in Revenue)
63%	47%	63%
27%	36%	28%
10%	17%	9%

☐ Excellent   ▨ Average   ■ Poor

exciting, when compared to the perceptions of the academics, they showed that these executives are somewhat more optimistic about their own current and future performance.

The survey participants were asked their opinions concerning the major environmental factors in government and society that are affecting their competitiveness, both at home and abroad (Figure A-11). Their responses were widely dispersed over several categories, including cost of capital, availability of qualified employees, labor costs, and government regulations. Many of the executives rated the pressure for short-term profits as a serious barrier to long-term company performance. But there was no strong consensus around any one or two factors, and no apparent conviction that the external environment was largely responsible for their competitive difficulties.

Next, we asked these executives about the primary bases for competition in their industries today and five years from now (Figures A-12 and A-13). These are the factors against which they must measure their performance to determine how competitive they really are. Here there were some differences in the answers between smaller companies or business

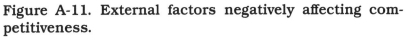

Figure A-11. External factors negatively affecting competitiveness.

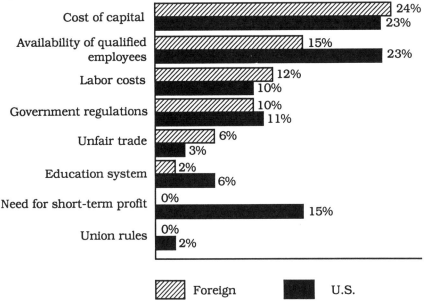

Cost of capital	24% / 23%
Availability of qualified employees	15% / 23%
Labor costs	12% / 10%
Government regulations	10% / 11%
Unfair trade	6% / 3%
Education system	2% / 6%
Need for short-term profit	0% / 15%
Union rules	0% / 2%

Foreign   U.S.

units (revenues of less than $1 billion) (Figure A-13) and larger ones whose revenue is greater than $1 billion (Figure A-12). In the smaller companies, executives believed that cost is now the primary basis, but in five years quality will take over as the leading one. The larger companies already showed a greater emphasis on quality over cost, and in five years, the emphasis on quality will become even stronger. Technical advances were rated third in priority. Shorter development cycles will be given far greater emphasis in five years than they are today, particularly by the larger companies.

We asked the participants in the survey to rate their products relative to their competition in a number of categories (Figure A-14). Despite the fact that these executives rated the primary bases for competition as cost and quality, slightly less than half rated their products above their competition in these categories. Then we asked them to rate the effectiveness of their product designs in meeting their objectives (Figure A-15). These executives rated their products high on aesthetics, reliability, and satisfying customer needs.

Figure A-12. Large-company executives' evaluation of primary bases for competition.

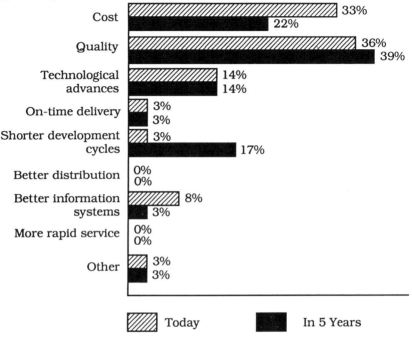

However, on manufacturing-related issues such as manufacturability, shorter development cycles, and cost, they gave themselves low marks.

When these executives evaluated their own manufacturing operations, they became even more critical. We asked them to rate their current manufacturing performance on a number of categories from "world class" to "unsatisfactory" (Figure A-16). Their number of world-class ratings was surprisingly low, and on many of the issues, specifically the development/manufacturing interface, cost, and new product launches, only 16 percent or less rated themselves world class. On the category labeled "new product launches," 41 percent rated their operations unsatisfactory. The fact that most of these executives held the key manufacturing positions in their respective companies makes these critical self-evaluations even more significant.

Where will these executives invest in the future to solve

Figure A-13. Small-company executives' evaluation of primary bases for competition.

Cost
40%
20%
Quality
25%
39%
Technological advances
12%
16%
On-time delivery
6%
9%
Shorter development cycles
4%
6%
Better distribution
3%
3%
Better information systems
2%
3%
More rapid service
0%
4%
Other
8%
0%
Today
In 5 Years

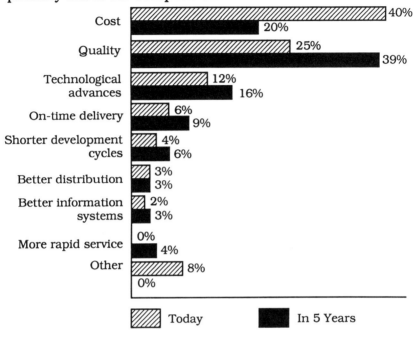

Figure A-14. Product ratings relative to foreign competition.

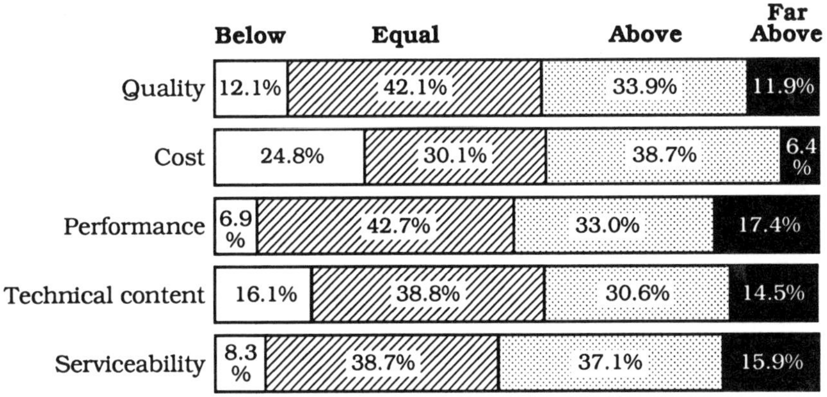

Below
Equal
Above
Far Above
Quality
12.1%
42.1%
33.9%
11.9%
Cost
24.8%
30.1%
38.7%
6.4 %
Performance
6.9 %
42.7%
33.0%
17.4%
Technical content
16.1%
38.8%
30.6%
14.5%
Serviceability
8.3 %
38.7%
37.1%
15.9%

Figure A-15. Effectiveness of product design process.

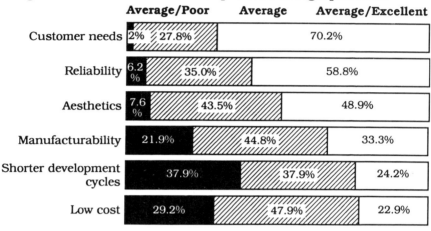

	Average/Poor	Average	Average/Excellent
Customer needs	2% / 27.8%		70.2%
Reliability	6.2% / 35.0%		58.8%
Aesthetics	7.6% / 43.5%		48.9%
Manufacturability	21.9%	44.8%	33.3%
Shorter development cycles	37.9%	37.9%	24.2%
Low cost	29.2%	47.9%	22.9%

Figure A-16. Rating manufacturing operations.

	Unsatisfactory	Adequate	World Class
Quality	8%	67%	25%
Cost, cost reduction	27%	59%	14%
Ability to handle mix and variety	13%	50%	37%
Ability to manage fluctuating demand	24%	45%	31%
Labor/management relations	13%	56%	31%
Product development, manufacturing interfaces	28%	62%	10%
Professional/ technical staff	12%	57%	31%
Capital equipment	21%	57%	22%
Manufacturing capability	14%	62%	24%
Work force capability/ experience	9%	70%	21%
New product launches	41%	43%	16%
Response to design changes	20%	64%	16%

some of their competitive problems (Figure A-17)? The executives plan to concentrate a major part of their future investment in total quality programs and capital equipment. They will invest the least in Just-In-Time (JIT) programs, automation, and computer systems. To shorten their development cycles, these executives will give most of their emphasis to integrated design teams; they will give least emphasis to technology tools such as CIM and CAD/CAM are near the bottom (Figure A-18).

Conclusions

What can we conclude from these data? Do the two groups agree or disagree? The members of academe are obviously quite pessimistic about the state of U.S. industry. The executives we polled are more optimistic concerning their own companies' competitive status and the prospects for the future. But even these less gloomy ratings of their companies' overall performance do not constitute a ringing endorsement of the

Figure A-17. Investing to meet future challenges.

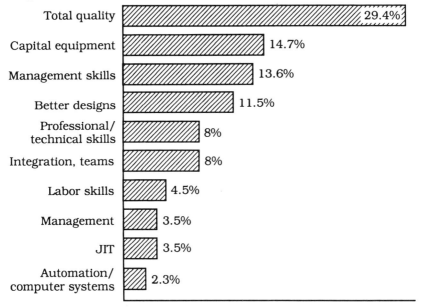

Figure A-18. Factors for shortening the development cycle.

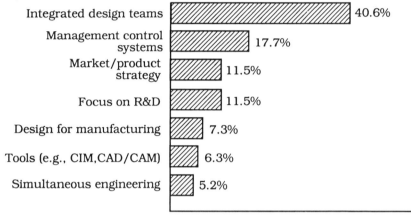

success of U.S. industry. Furthermore, many of the executives' answers to questions concerning detailed performance told an even less optimistic story.

There are areas of significant agreement between the two groups:

- Neither group claims that U.S. industry is in a commanding position of worldwide leadership.
- Neither group ascribes our industrial problems solely to governmental and societal factors.
- Both groups rate manufacturing rather low in its contribution to competitiveness.
- Both groups strongly recommend changes in corporate structures, with emphasis on organizational integration and teams with manufacturing as an equal partner.
- Both groups gave very low ratings to the success that technology tools and Just-In-Time programs have achieved to date.

There is clearly a considerable degree of agreement among these professors and executives that U.S. industry has serious problems and that major change is necessary to solve them. Based on these interviews and surveys, during the late

1990s and beyond, the primary emphasis of companies will be on higher quality, lower cost, technology advances, and rapid movement of new technologies and products to the marketplace. The emphasis on all these objectives is completely consistent with and supportive of the technical and organizational directions this book has proposed. The fundamental problems that prevent companies from achieving each of these goals, as well as their solutions, are common to all of them. The steps on the critical path to shorter product development cycles that this book has discussed will go a long way toward meeting these objectives and making U.S. industry competitive again.

Appendix B

Case Studies: How Different Companies Manage the Product Cycle

Corning Incorporated

Corning is an international corporation with revenues totaling $3 billion. It focuses on four business areas: specialty materials, telecommunications, laboratory services, and consumer products. Corning is a household name and, depending on the household, is well known for its Corning Ware cookware and Steuben glass. But its product line spreads well beyond, to test tubes and laboratory beakers, ultra-flat TV glass, glass-ceramic tooth replacement material, cellular ceramic technology for diesel engine filters, and photochromatic eyeglass lenses that darken in the sunlight. One of Corning's most profitable businesses is glass fiber for optical wave guides for the telecommunications industry. Corning produces about 60 percent of the total market for this product.

Corning's products are technology- and material-based and involve a great deal of scientific knowledge. Because of its need to bridge the gap between science, technology, production, and the requirements of the marketplace, Corning has historically placed great emphasis on a strong technical organization. Many of its top executives are trained engineers and scientists. At the core of these efforts is the Corning Technology Group situated in Corning, New York, where the total

production process—from research through engineering—
has been combined under a common management. There are
1,200 people in this group; approximately half are in research
and development (R&D) and half in engineering.

Corning bases its business on a strong scientific foundation, and it fosters strong fundamental and applied research
activities to provide this foundation. Corning is convinced
that the only way to be at the "cutting edge" of new products
is to make a firm commitment to research. But it also stresses
that money for R&D alone is not enough. Consequently, there
is a great deal of emphasis on how technical resources are
allocated and integrated into the business. One important
step Corning has taken is to tie its research activities closely
to the subsequent development and engineering operations.

The Corning organization can be illustrated by following
the development of one of its products from the research laboratory to manufacturing: the development of a glass-ceramic
product for use in food-preparation and storage containers.
The research laboratory experiments with a ceramic material
with such characteristics as porosity, a foam glaze, good insulation properties, light weight, and durability after repeated
cleaning in automatic dishwashers. Research formulates such
a material and determines that it has these properties. At this
point, the process is transferred to development to design the
optimum and lowest-cost method of making it. Marketing determines its marketability and tests it in the field.

The manufacturing engineers join the program very
early in the development period. Their role is to assess the
product from the point of view of its ultimate manufacturability and to answer such questions as the effect of the glass
chemistry on the surface of the molds. Corning has learned
from experience that bringing these engineers into the development process and having the total research, development,
marketing, and manufacturing engineering activities work in
a closely knit team, from the very beginning, are essential.
Before it adopted this type of organization, Corning was constantly "building itself into a box."

Despite this rigorous approach to research and development, Corning still experiences unanticipated technical problems even after the product has been introduced into the

marketplace and even though it was convinced that it knew all it needed to know about the materials and processes. One example is the sudden discovery of the adverse effect of humidity on the yield and quality of one of the ceramic products during manufacturing (discussed in Chapter 5).

Teamwork among the major parts of the company, including research, is clearly an important factor in Corning's position in the glass industry. But making trade-offs between the product design and the manufacturing process is not the only reason that this organizational integration is working at Corning. There are many other important technical and business issues that require the intensive cooperation of the technology, marketing, and manufacturing groups. For example:

• Has research checked to ensure that none of the materials proposed is carcinogenic or toxic?
• What type of patent protection can be obtained with a new invention?
• Where is the best location to build a new plant, considering such vital questions as labor supply and distribution and transportation patterns?
• When is the right time to make major investment decisions?

All these technical and business decisions require the intensive involvement of the triumvirate of technology, manufacturing, and marketing. Corning considers these three arms equivalent to a three-legged stool—the system will not work if one of the legs is missing.

In summary, three of the important keys to Corning's leadership position are the heavy emphasis on technology, a strong technical base for its products, and very close integration of the technical, marketing, and manufacturing activities.

Although Corning management cannot yet prove that this type of integration has led to a measurable reduction in the length of the product cycle, it is convinced that integration has definitely increased its rate of success.

DuPont Medical Products and Imaging Systems

The DuPont Medical Products Department makes several specialized products for the medical industry including diagnostic instruments and biotechnology systems as well as centrifuges and radioactive chemicals for research institutions and universities.

The Imaging Systems Department serves three major markets: the printing and publishing business with photographic films, graphic arts films, printing plates, and proofing products; diagnostic imaging with films for chest x-rays; and industrial imaging, including nondestructive testing and x-rays to determine the quality of welds on pipes.

In these divisions, DuPont is making some significant changes in organization that it believes will greatly strengthen its product development and introduction programs. All research and development is under the direction of one vice-president. A small central R&D group studies new business initiatives and new technologies. The bulk of the R&D effort is decentralized by business and aligned at several manufacturing locations. At each location, a joint "product introduction team" (PIT) is formed with members from both the R&D group and the manufacturing plant. As the program approaches production scale-up, more manufacturing people join the team, but there is no intermediate engineering organization and no "hand-offs." The total integrated technical program from research to production remains in the hands of this team.

Furthermore, DuPont has broken down many of the traditional barriers and caste hierarchies that characterize most technical organizations. Although the R&D component of the team generally is composed of many people with doctorates in chemistry, and the manufacturing people tend to be chemical and mechanical engineers, there is no real distinction between the two populations in terms of technical training and competence. In fact, the total group is referred to as the "technical community"; DuPont has melded the two organizations into one.

Although DuPont instituted this practice several years ago and is incorporating it in many parts of the company, it does have some problems making it work as effectively as it would like. One of the most serious difficulties arises from the lack of stability of the team membership. Because people are frequently transferred to other jobs, it is difficult to keep the team unit together. According to the vice-president of research and development, "you lose time every time someone moves out." In addition, the only people who are really full-time members originate from the R&D function. Since the manufacturing and marketing representatives have other jobs and responsibilities, they are not dedicated to a single program. This problem is considered a major issue by DuPont management, which is working on ways to solve it.

DuPont is putting a lot of emphasis on integrating its research and development efforts into the business process. In the past, the business management team did not get involved in product development until late in the cycle. Today, product development is involved in the business process very early, so that when decisions are made on new products, the research and development organizations are in a much better position to influence those decisions.

In the past, DuPont believes it has been too aggressive in incorporating too many significant changes simultaneously in a new product. Partly because of its deserved reputation as an innovative company, DuPont has emphasized major improvements in new products. After a new product program was launched, research and marketing would often recommend additional improvements and changes even as the design cycle progressed. The effect of these changes, as well as the risk involved in incorporating too many of them at once, created significant schedule slippages. Benchmarking studies of other leading companies convinced DuPont management that one of the keys to shortening the product cycle was to limit the advances incorporated in a single product and to freeze the product concept at the beginning of the cycle. DuPont is trying to institute a disciplined process to do just that. Instead of introducing several changes in one product, it carefully plans on incorporating them over a sequence of several products. Not only does this reduce the risk, it enables the company to concentrate on product design "robustness," design for manufacturability, and the use of Taguchi experimental design techniques.

Since this strategy is relatively new, its effect cannot be quantified yet, but DuPont projects a 40 percent reduction in the length of the product cycle from this mode of operation. In summary, DuPont Imaging Systems is incorporating several changes that it expects will make significant improvements in the length of the product development cycle. It is linking product development much closer to business strategy and doing it much earlier in the product cycle. It is decentralizing research and development and tying them closely to individual businesses. It is strengthening the relationships between research and development and manufacturing using product introduction teams and eliminating some of the distinctions between research, development, and manufacturing engineers. Finally, DuPont is adopting a strategy of more incremental and fewer simultaneous advances in one product and giving more emphasis to product design robustness.

Eastman Kodak Company, Copy Products Division

The Copy Products Division of Eastman Kodak is a self-contained, integrated business unit. Its organization spans the spectrum of research, development, manufacturing, marketing, service, planning, and finance. When strategic decisions are made on which products and technologies to pursue, all functions are included. Even manufacturing becomes involved very early when the first business case is developed as part of a total research, development, and manufacturing team.

The division manufactures most of its own products, including color copiers and electronic printers, as well as toner, developer, film, and fuser rollers. It buys components and raw materials such as sheet metal, castings, and circuit boards from suppliers within or outside Kodak.

One of the first issues Kodak Copy must address is the length of its product cycle. And one of the most difficult aspects of that assessment is deciding how many new technologies should be involved in a new product. In the past, it encountered serious problems by attempting too many new technologies simultaneously. The decision is complicated by the fact that it is not always clear what constitutes a new advance or how large an advance really is. Nevertheless, there is general agreement that Kodak Copy should introduce less technology change than it has in the past and limit such changes to no more than several at one time. It considers a good portfolio of products to consist of two or three new technologies and two or three products that are "leveraged" from older products.

Kodak Copy tries to build prototypes as early as possible in the cycle. The first phase of the cycle is called Phase 0, when the technology is certified as "ready." At this point, a breadboard is built for each of the principal subsystems of the product. During this phase, issues of basic physics are often involved, and it is premature to put the subsystems together and test them as a total system. However, at Phase I, which occurs approximately six months later, a stage of "system readiness" is reached and a total integrated system is built. In the past, Kodak Copy has waited too long before carrying out these two tests. Consequently, it has discovered some basic problems late in the cycle and has had to go back and redo much of the design work. It is now giving much more emphasis to the earliest systems integration and testing.

Because of the complexity of the copier products and the close interactions between the subsystems, problems can be created by operating at or beyond the limits of the technologies involved. As a result, Kodak is stressing "robustness" of design. In the past, it carried out an analysis of each subsystem to determine the measurement tolerances that would be necessary for the total system to work. If the total system worked with these tolerances, the design was satisfactory. Under the concept of robustness, Kodak now examines the limits where the designs *do not* work, extending the limits beyond the specifications to determine where the system will fail. Operating conditions can change with age of the equipment and the customer environment if specifications move beyond the limits. By examining the designs until they fail, Kodak is able to determine their limits.

Manufacturing is brought into the development process

very early. In essence, the practice of concurrent engineering is begun in the research laboratory. Even before the design begins, when the laboratory is exploring the technology and systems concepts and trying to prove technology readiness, at least one manufacturing engineer is assigned to work on the project. He or she will eventually lead a larger manufacturing team as the program progresses. In essence, the study of manufacturability actually begins this early. Kodak Copy defines "design" as taking a mechanical or electrical concept that has been demonstrated in a raw technology breadboard form and converting it to a manufacturable design. Even at this early stage of the evolution of the product, the manufacturing engineers begin to study the basic requirements necessary for the product to work. They even begin to make some basic manufacturing decisions on the selection of materials, where certain functions of the machine should be placed physically, and which suppliers can make some critical components, such as a transfer roller with the necessary electrostatic and conductive properties. Through Kodak's Early Supplier Involvement Program (ESIP), the supplier also participates in this early part of the design process.

Kodak is working to upgrade its manufacturing engineering staff. In the past, these engineers had a lower status than their design or research counterparts. Kodak is trying, with some success, to change that by attracting technical people with higher skills from both within and outside Kodak. Also, many of the design people make the transition with the product to manufacturing as production begins. This encourages the interchange of both manufacturing and product design expertise.

In summary, the Kodak Copy Division is stressing four important changes in the way it has run its business in the past in order to shorten and increase the rate of success of the product cycle:

1. It is pursuing a more incremental product strategy and is more careful about the degree of change in each product generation.
2. It integrates and tests prototype systems much earlier than in the past, and gives great emphasis to thorough analysis of these prototypes.

3. It is integrating research, development, and manufacturing early in the program; it is maintaining that integration throughout the product cycle, including the use of concurrent engineering.
4. Through ESIP, it is concentrating on earlier and more intensive involvement of suppliers in the product cycle.

Kodak Copy management believes that it is too early to measure the effect of all these measures on the length of the product cycle, but it is confident that Kodak is beginning to see a greater success rate in new product programs.

Abbott Laboratories, Diagnostic Products Division

The Abbott Diagnostic Division researches, develops, and markets diagnostic products worldwide in the areas of immunodiagnostics, clinical chemistry, and physicians' office/alternative care. Its products and its system of managing the product cycle provide an interesting subject because of the nature of the technology. Many of Abbott's diagnostic products consist of the integration of mechanical and optical systems with chemistry. This integration presents some major scientific, technical, and manufacturing challenges. An illustration of these challenges is the example (Chapter 5) of the Abbott product that quickly analyzes a patient's blood chemistry in the doctor's office.

There are essentially three levels of research upon which Abbott depends for its products. The first level—the discovery of a new marker and the association of that marker with a specific disease—often comes out of public or private universities. The second level of research is carried out in a central divisional research and development laboratory that explores long-range new products. The remainder of the division's research and development activities have been decentralized by business unit. These activities focus on products that will be manufactured during the next few years. Consequently, each business unit includes the entire spectrum of technical activities.

A major constituent of diagnostic products is a reagent, a

substance that is used to create a chemical reaction to detect and measure other substances. A considerable amount of research is required to determine the merit of different reagents when studying new methods of detecting diseases. In the cases of well-known diseases such as hepatitis B, selecting and refining reagents is quite simple. But in the case of lesser-known diseases such as hepatitis C, where current tests need considerable improvement, much more research is necessary to find the right reagent. A key part of the process of studying these reagents is the interface with clinics and physicians, since they have well-documented clinical patient histories. Consequently, these physicians and medical clinics become part of the development process.

Abbott is emphasizing several aspects of the research and development of its products in order to shorten the cycle time to market. First, the company is focusing on minimizing the technical risk in new programs and maximizing the probability of delivering the critical features of new products. This involves a combination of understanding the marketplace on the one hand and the technical risks on the other. To do this, it uses proven technology as much as possible.

Next, Abbott is trying to establish a combination of design goals very early and obtain a firm commitment to achieving these goals from every organization, including research and development, manufacturing, and marketing. In the past, when it did not obtain this firm commitment and focus on these goals from the very beginning, it encountered unnecessary delays.

Abbott has been working with integrated teams since the early 1980s, and it is convinced that this mode of operation is far more effective than the old functional organization. This integration is particularly important in its type of product, which involves a complex marriage between the hardware and the reagents. Integration is paying off in better product performance, lower cost, and shorter cycles.

Caterpillar, Inc.

Caterpillar, Inc., is a world leader in the manufacture of construction equipment and heavy-duty engines and trucks. Situated in Peoria, Illinois, it is technologically far from the

Rust Belt. Caterpillar's products are complex high-technology systems, and the development and manufacture of these systems in a highly competitive market demand an aggressive approach to product development and manufacturing.

The heart of Caterpillar's product development cycle is a formalized process called New Product Introduction (NPI). The system consists of several well-defined phases or generations. It defines a schedule for each generation and closely monitors it. Each generation represents a stage of development. Depending on how many new product features are added, the number of generations ranges from two to four. The first is the concept stage; the subsequent generations are called experimental, preproduction, and production.

A major element in the management system is concurrent product and process development (CPPD), which brings design and manufacturing engineers together very early in the design stage. In the past, manufacturing never became associated with a new product until late in the development cycle. Consequently, designs could be adopted that contained excessive cost features. Although the CPPD process in various forms is achieving considerable success, one of the barriers to the most effective use of this concept is the lack of skilled manufacturing engineers available in the marketplace. Engineers with these special skills are difficult to find, and they are badly needed in a company that is at the leading edge of technology in its field.

Caterpillar is very careful about the magnitude of technology advancement it incorporates into new products and the degree of risk it adopts. It uses two criteria to assess and control this risk factor: (1) the new product content (the percentage of the overall product that embodies new components), and (2) the number of major inventions (totally new technology for the product involved).

Whenever a new feature is introduced—for example, a change in transmission design, a different engine configuration, a higher power level, or a redesigned operator station— a separate test and development program is set up for it in the laboratory. During the experimental phase, Caterpillar integrates the entire product, placing the greatest emphasis on incorporating these new features. The main objectives of this generation are to prove that the product functions satisfactorily and to identify and solve problems. During the next generation, in addition to continuing the process of refining the design of the product, Caterpillar begins to demonstrate the reliability of the product. The company claims that it has a process of validating product reliability that is second to none.

An important basis for Caterpillar's high product reliability is its policy that every new product must be as good as or better than the one it is replacing, beginning with the first models off the production line. Since each new product consists of a number of new features and production processes, achieving this goal is difficult. In order to meet this objective, Caterpillar institutes a rigorous regimen of testing at each prototype stage. In many companies, the first models of a new product off the assembly line have more defects than the old product it is replacing. Then after the manufacturer discovers and finally removes many of the defects, the reliability of the product begins to approach and eventually exceed that of its predecessor. Caterpillar is following a different course. The first buyers of its new products experience equal or better reliability than they were getting with their old models. To do this, Caterpillar tests preproduction prototypes under severe conditions in order to accelerate the discovery of any failure modes as rapidly as possible. It has designed tests that will equate the number of hours under extreme operating conditions with the number of hours under normal conditions. With these tests, Caterpillar can find defects early and fix them before customer exposure.

Next, after the manufacturing line is installed, fifteen or twenty more models are built. These represent the most updated manufacturing processes and also most closely simulate production conditions. These models are tested by select customers, and their performance is closely monitored. By taking these steps, Caterpillar is able to detect and remove defects and failure modes well before the product reaches the marketplace.

But despite this rigorous development and testing program as well as the early prototype integration of the total system, it is still possible for Caterpillar to encounter unexpected problems after the customer begins to operate the equipment. At this point, Caterpillar engineers try to discover why these problems were not found earlier in the design and analysis phase. One common answer is that the customer is using the product in a way the company had not foreseen—for example, on an excessively steep grade. Consequently, the customer interface is an important part of the development process for this type of heavy equipment.

In summary, Caterpillar's management system for the introduction of new products includes these features:

- A formal new product introduction process
- Thorough analysis of the number and magnitude of technical advances and inventions introduced into a new product
- Early integration of the total product and incorporation of new features to assess the interactions of the subsystems
- Close linkage of the product design and manufacturing process using concurrent product and process development
- A strong reliability program to ensure the superiority of each new product over the previous one
- A strong tie to the customer throughout the process, from the early concept phase through the final stage of production

Stanley Magic-Door

Stanley Magic-Door, a subsidiary of The Stanley Works, manufactures automatic sliding doors—the automatic swinging doors we pass through at the supermarket—and parking systems, including ticket dispensers and barrier gates that greet us at the airport parking lot. The company has its main plant in Connecticut and also operates plants in England and Italy.

Stanley Magic-Door is in a very competitive field. Product life cycles are shrinking, and time to market is becoming very important. In the past, it could maintain a product in the marketplace for at least five years. Today, that cycle has decreased to two years. This means that shortly after introducing a product, Stanley must prepare to replace it with a new and more advanced one. As soon as a design is released to manufacturing, the engineers begin to design the next generation of products. This continuous change places a great deal of pressure on the costs of Stanley's products.

Each time Stanley begins to descend the learning curve and approach its cost projections for a new product, the investment in the development of the next product raises the curve again. Stanley's solution to this moving target is to accelerate the learning process and achieve higher productivity from the very beginning of production. In order to achieve this rapid learning rate, Stanley has taken a number of measures, including:

• Decreasing the levels in its manufacturing management hierarchy by integrating the materials and engineering groups into production operations. The manufacturing engineering and materials people report directly to one of three production managers, who in turn report to the plant manager. At the same time, Stanley has eliminated staff functions and placed all its manufacturing employees on the factory floor with direct responsibility for manufacturing the product.

• Coordinating design activities more closely with marketing in order to get direct input from the customers and thus be more responsive to their needs. Stanley believes that the time wasted in redesign because of lack of coordination with the marketplace can be longer than the original project itself.

• Rotating personnel through product engineering, manufacturing, and marketing to give them broader experience.

• Upgrading the skill level of manufacturing engineers and assigning them to design teams very early so that they can develop the manufacturing processes and play an active role in the design of the product. However, Stanley, like many other companies, is finding it difficult to persuade qualified engineers to take jobs in manufacturing rather than in the more glamorous field of product design. The company is also handicapped by a dearth of manufacturing engineers possessing the high level of skills needed to participate on an equal footing with design engineers.

Stanley buys most of the components used in its products from outside suppliers. When a component is particularly critical and its level of quality important, Stanley concentrates on the development of a very close working relationship with the suppliers. One example is the aluminum used for its glass doors. Since that is the only part of the product visible to the customer, the maintenance of high quality and the prevention of shading or streaking are extremely important. The company uses a single vendor for this item. Stanley maintains a close relationship with the vendor, which dedicates a number of presses exclusively for Stanley's products. Other critical components are the precision gears and gear boxes that are used with the motors that drive Stanley's products. Stanley designs these gears and then subcontracts their manufacture to outside suppliers. One exception to Stanley's policy of purchasing components is the infrared sensing device for automatic swinging doors, which it designs and manufactures itself. Stanley made this exception because of the very critical nature of this component and its importance to the company's competitive position. The infrared sensor and Stanley's decision to build it are discussed in more detail in Chapter 8. In addition, even though Stanley purchases electronic circuits from suppliers, it actually designs some of its more unique and critical circuits itself.

Another interesting aspect of Stanley Magic-Door's policies is its view on the use of new technology and the rate at which it is introduced into new products. Stanley is driven more by market need than the appeal of technology. Stanley management does not believe in using technology for the sake of technology itself, particularly if the marketplace does not require it. Everything engineering develops does not necessarily need to be used in a new product. Nevertheless, Stanley is willing to invest in engineering to continue to advance technology, evaluate its potential in the marketplace, and then decide on its future use.

David Sarnoff Research Center, Subsidiary of SRI International

The David Sarnoff Research Center at Princeton, New Jersey, a subsidiary of SRI International and formerly a part of the Radio Corporation of America, has a distinguished record of innovation, including the invention of color television and liquid crystal displays as well as the earliest development of complementary metal oxide semiconductor (CMOS) transistors. The current mission of the Sarnoff laboratories is the creation and application of innovative technology and service to industry and government. The primary orientation is still the electronics industry; Sarnoff specializes in solid-state devices, displays, computer vision, digital video, and software development. It also has sizable activity in enhanced and high-definition television.

Approximately 40 percent of its business is devoted to the U.S. Government and another 40 percent to Thomson Electric; the remainder is research carried out for U.S.-based and Far East clients. Sarnoff management classifies most of its activities as applied research, although its work for the U.S. Government tends to be more basic.

Sarnoff exemplifies some of the problems as well as the opportunities in the application of applied research to the development of new products. These problems are due to the difficulty of gaining client acceptance of the research laboratory's work. This occurs whenever there is a physical and organizational separation between the two operations, particularly if the research laboratory, like Sarnoff, is a separate company. Sarnoff management points out that the only way the results of its research will be utilized effectively is if someone at the receiving end is committed to that use. In fact, the performance of the client's engineers must be measured by how they actually incorporate the research results into the development of the product. Sarnoff states that "their paycheck must depend upon it." Otherwise, the research results culminate in a report or a published article and are then relegated to a shelf and forgotten.

Further aggravating the difficulty companies have in

capitalizing on the knowledge gained from research laboratories is the relationship between the laboratory and the engineering recipients of the research output. These engineers
often consider the research scientists as competitors and may
even have a vested interest in their failure rather than their
success. This problem may exist even though some higher-
level manager may be strongly supportive of Sarnoff's work.

Sarnoff recognizes these problems and is continually
trying to solve them. It has identified several keys to the creation of a successful relationship with clients who receive and
exploit its research results. One key is the nature of the work
produced. SRI does not believe in "writing papers and walk-
ing away." After carrying out initial feasibility studies, which
sometimes extend for several years, the research laboratory
delivers "total solutions," including hardware and software
prototypes. It then continues to support the further development of the product throughout the product design and into
manufacturing by maintaining close communication with
customers. Another key to successful acceptance of its work is
the effort to get clients to "own" the final results. By including
clients in the early conceptualizing of a new product, even to
the point of having them play a major part in its creation,
Sarnoff can establish this sense of client ownership, an important factor in achieving success in applying research to a
client's products.

Direct interaction between Sarnoff and its clients is very
important. Frequent visits to the laboratories by client engineering personnel are encouraged, and Sarnoff has actually
housed client personnel for as long as six months at the
Princeton site. Despite the advantages of this continual client
presence, there are problems with security of information if
too many clients are free to circulate at the same time. Sarnoff
is considering reserving a portion of the laboratory buildings
for visiting clients and limiting access to the other parts of
the laboratories.

Sarnoff has a strong contingent of experts on a wide
range of materials. It believes that this type of knowledge is
priceless, not only in contributing to the development of new
products and processes, but also in assisting the factory in
diagnosing and solving materials problems. Sarnoff believes

that the development of a new product must consist of a sizable effort to intensively test new materials in order to understand their behavior and to diagnose and solve every possible problem that may occur in their use. But it also believes that it is impossible to ensure that all such problems are solved in the research stage. It states that "you can't possibly begin to imagine the kind of things that happen in the real world when you start producing large quantities of a new product." For that reason, Sarnoff experts, well grounded in the fundamentals of materials, have been instrumental in working with their clients' manufacturing personnel, assisting them in interpreting strange phenomena and diagnosing and solving troublesome problems that erupt on the factory floor.

Sarnoff management believes that the application of new materials to new products should follow this sequence:

1. Simulate as closely as possible how the new materials will behave in the product.
2. Gain as much basic understanding of the composition and behavior of the materials as possible.
3. Have available the best technical expertise to assist the factory in diagnosing and solving the inevitable problems that will arise.

How much impact does a strong applied research program and good integration with the client's development program have on the length of the product development cycle? According to Sarnoff management, its experience indicates that although there may be some effect on the cycle length, the primary impact is on the probability of success of the product program. The stronger the research and the coupling with the receiving client's development program, the greater the chances for that success.

Analog Devices

Analog Devices Incorporated (ADI) is a major manufacturer of analog integrated circuits, assembled products, and subsystems for application in precision measurement and control systems. It has an annual revenue in excess of $500 million and manufactures its products in eight locations. Half of its products are used in industrial and instrumentation applications, and the remainder are sold to military, avionics, and computer markets.

ADI generally follows an incremental product strategy—each new product generation represents incremental rather than revolutionary change from the previous one. It performs no research itself, but follows closely the fruits of research from other companies and academic institutions. It relies heavily on innovativeness in design and a very strong engineering staff.

During the 1970s and early 1980s, ADI's sales grew at a 27 percent annual rate. But then its rate of increase slowed to about 8 to 9 percent. This slower rate is at least partially explained by a comparable slowdown in the growth rate of its primary customers, including Hewlett-Packard and IBM. Another interesting fact is that ADI is introducing new products at a comparable rate of approximately 7 percent a year. Assuming that each new product has approximately the same life cycle, ADI would need to introduce products at a faster rate to achieve a higher growth in revenue. Consequently, ADI must give greater emphasis to shortening the development cycle, which has remained constant over the years.

Although ADI's recent growth in new product introductions has been much slower than in the past, its investment in research and development by percentage of revenue has actually been climbing, from 9 percent in 1984 to 17 percent in 1990. The gap between the rate of generation of new products and expenditures in R&D indicates that the company is not getting a good return on its R&D investment.

There is another important factor that will determine the course of ADI's business and how it is managed in the future. Although historically ADI has been the leader in linear integrated circuits, its competition has not been very strong. Today, many of the applications that once used totally linear circuitry are being designed with a mixture of linear and digital circuits—called "mixed signal." Because of this change, ADI is beginning to compete with many other strong companies such as Motorola, Texas Instruments, and National

Semiconductor. Where ADI formerly played a dominant role in linear circuitry, it must now compete with major manufacturers of digital circuits. In other words, this change in technology is having a great impact on ADI's competitive environment.

Consequently, ADI faces two major challenges: a major redirection of technology, and the need to expand its markets and increase the rate of generation of new products for those markets. In order to expedite its product cycle and move more products to market, ADI is taking several steps:

• It is moving to consolidate a very decentralized company to one far more centralized. This centralization is intended to make the decision-making process more visible and efficient. Today there are eight autonomous divisions competing with one another. In Europe alone, ADI has thirteen autonomous general sales managers. All these autonomous activities will be consolidated into three groups that will not be competing for the same markets. Furthermore, ADI intends to present one face to its customers. For greater efficiency, it also plans to centralize manufacturing and quality assurance.

• The manner in which ADI is moving toward centralization is actually consistent with the trend of other companies that are decentralizing to shorten their product development cycle. Much of the decentralization of larger companies with several product lines is to achieve greater focus on each individual product. Since ADI develops and markets one fairly homogeneous product line, its new organization will bring together the fragments essential for more effectively managing that line. And the company organization will look more like the individual, decentralized, product-oriented business units of these larger companies.

• In order to speed the development cycle, ADI is taking steps to bring the product designers and manufacturers much closer together and give greater emphasis to design for manufacturability. Like many high-technology companies, ADI is highly engineering-dominated. Because of this domination and other cultural differences between engineering and manufacturing, these changes will present major challenges to the company.

• ADI is working to build very close relationships with its customers. First, close relationships are built at the executive levels. For example, ADI executives attend quarterly meetings of purchasing and quality people from both ADI and client companies to gain an understanding of both parties' needs and capabilities. Teams are formed with engineers from both companies, who communicate with one another on a daily basis. Design engineers from the customer actually come to ADI, sit down with the ADI engineers, and look at ADI simulations. The working relationship is so close that they feel like they are working for the same company. These steps toward supplier-customer integration have greatly increased customer confidence in ADI and have led to an increase in customer demand for ADI products. Accomplishing this type of supplier-customer integration is not easy. There is much resistance to it on both sides. But it has worked very well in some instances, and ADI management would like to extend this model to relationships with other suppliers.

• ADI is recognizing that the complexity of its business requires that top executives become directly involved in driving the management process. This is essential to ensure that the coordination of all functions be carried out smoothly to achieve the objective of total quality. Furthermore, ADI management must assure that the proper trade-offs are made between short-term and long-term investments and objectives. In the past, top management of ADI, like the management of most corporations in the United States, delegated this role to lower levels. Because of past practices and corporate culture, changing to this mode of greater involvement and direct management will not be easy.

Analog Devices is a successful company and a leader in its field. But technology and the bases for competition are changing rapidly, presenting some significant challenges. ADI's efforts to achieve more top management involvement, greater functional integration within the company, and a higher degree of integration with customers are all important steps it must take to maintain its leadership position.

The Burndy Corporation

The Burndy Corporation is a major supplier of electrical connectors with manufacturing and sales operations in every principal geographical market throughout the world. It is a leading supplier of integrated circuit sockets and connectors for several blue-chip electronics companies. In Europe Burndy is a major supplier to the telecommunications industry and is increasing its penetration of the transportation and automotive market. Its worldwide annual revenue is approximately $385 million. Over half of its sales are products used for electronics applications.

The general perception of the electrical connector is that of a simple device consisting solely of an electrical conductor and a piece of plastic. That perception is hardly correct today. With the accelerating performance of computers and telecommunications equipment, the demands on connector technology are escalating rapidly. The connector must be essentially electrically invisible to the very high-speed electronic circuitry in these types of products. In order to achieve this performance at low costs, today's connectors require insulating plastic materials of high mechanical stability under high temperature processing conditions as well as new methods of gold and nickel plating.

These connectors are used not only for repair and replacement of defective components on a circuit board, but also as manufacturing aids. The advances made in contact technology, although not revolutionary from year to year, involve very difficult and challenging improvements in processes. Because of the shrinking of electronic circuitry, the size of the connectors must also decrease. With this trend toward size reduction, placing these connectors onto the boards with machines such as robots becomes a very challenging task. Today, Burndy is working with contact pitches of 50 mils. It claims that Japan has developed contacts as small as 25 mils. In order to work with such dimensions, it is exploring new etching and milling processes.

Because of these technology and product performance trends, and because the connector is becoming an increasingly intimate part of the electronic system, its development must be carried out very closely with the development of that system. Consequently, Burndy goes far beyond the traditional supplier-customer relationship. It becomes involved very early in the design cycle of its customers' equipment. Although the relationship begins at the executive and purchasing department levels, it rapidly passes to the engineers in both companies. Burndy works hard to build a high level of trust at all customer management levels. This trust greatly assists in forming a smooth and close relationship between engineers in the two companies. This engineering relationship is one of the major keys to Burndy's success.

In addition, Burndy encourages close bonds between its own design and manufacturing engineers. This relationship occurs through teams that are formed very early in the design of a new product, with representatives from both parties. Both parties serve on an equal basis and have the same level of skills. Helping to promulgate this relationship is the fact that design engineering as well as manufacturing and marketing are under the control of a business unit manager. Burndy, which has always been proud of its engineering strength, has fostered this type of team practice for at least thirty years.

Burndy management claims there have been circumstances when these tight relationships have resulted in products that rapidly moved directly from design to prototype to hard production tooling to satisfied customers with no iterations in the design. Of course, life is not always that easy, and it admits that this happy state of affairs is the exception, not the rule. Nevertheless, Burndy's record appears to prove that its mode of operation greatly improves development cycle time and has led to successful relationships with customers.

In summary, Burndy practices two levels of organizational integration, both of which this book has emphasized as essential for short product cycles, low cost, and high quality. The first level consists of the integration of Burndy as supplier and its customers; the second level is the integration of the Burndy engineers who design the connectors and those who will ultimately be responsible for converting those designs to manufacturable products.

Bibliography

Clark, Kim B., Robert H. Hayes, and Christopher Lorenz. *The Uneasy Alliance*. Boston: Harvard Business School Press, 1985.

Clark, Kim B., and Takahiro Fujimoto. *Product Development Performance: Strategy, Organization, and Management in the World Auto Industry*. Boston: Harvard Business School Press, 1991.

Cohen, Steven S., and John Zysman. *Manufacturing Matters*. New York: Basic Books, 1987.

Dertouzos, Michael L., Richard K. Lester, Robert M. Solow, and The MIT Commission on Industrial Productivity. *Made in America: Regaining the Productive Edge*. Cambridge, Mass.: MIT Press, 1989.

Foster, Richard. *Innovation*. New York: Summit Books, 1986.

Galbraith, John Kenneth. *The New Industrial State*. Boston: Houghton Mifflin, 1967.

Hayes, Robert H., Steven C. Wheelwright, and Kim B. Clark. *Dynamic Manufacturing*. New York: Free Press, 1988.

Keller, Mary Ann. *Rude Awakening*. New York: William Morrow and Co., 1989.

Morton, J. A. *Organizing for Innovation*. New York: McGraw-Hill, 1971.

Pugh, Emerson W., Lyle R. Johnson, and John H. Palmer. *IBM's 360 and Early 370 Systems*. Cambridge, Mass.: MIT Press, 1991.

Rosenau, Milton D., Jr. *Faster New Product Development*. New York: AMACOM, 1990.

Rosenthal, Stephen R. *Effective Product Design and Development: Cutting Lead Time and Increasing Customer Satisfaction*. Homewood, Ill.: Business One Irwin, 1992.

Slade, Bernard N., and Raj Mohindra. *Winning the Productivity Race*. Lexington, Mass.: Lexington Books, D.C. Heath and Company, 1985.

Stalk, George, Jr., and Thomas M. Hout. *Competing Against Time: How Time-Based Competition Is Reshaping Global Markets*. New York: Free Press, 1990.

Womack, James P., Daniel T. Jones, and Daniel Roos. *The Machine That Changed the World*. New York: Rawson Associates, 1990.

Index

Abbott Laboratories, 58, 194–195
Analog Devices, 125–126, 203–207
Anderson, Philip, analysis of technology change by, with Tushman, 14–15
applied research, 36, 56, 59–60, 65, 68
authority, program manager's, 33
automated production line, 78–79

basic research, 59
Beggs, James, 92
Bell Telephone Laboratories, 66
Boothroyd-Dewhurst, Inc., 84
breadboard, 100, 192
Burndy Corp., 125–126, 207–208

case studies, 186–208
Caterpillar, Inc., 195–198
change, 7, 45, 47–48, 174
    commitment to, 159–160
    evaluation methods for, 51–54
    and risks, 45
    see also technological change
Clark, Kim, study by, with Henderson, 17–19
collaboration, 10, 62–64, 126
communications, 149–154
competitiveness, 4, 13, 57, 87
    barriers to, 1
    foundation for, 56
    technological advance and, 44
complexity, 90
concurrent engineering, 80–82, 193

concurrent product and process development, 196
Corning Incorporated, 58, 65, 186–188
crisis management, 156
critical components, 113–117
    purchasing, 120–124
critical path, 5, 137, 155–163
customers, 36, 206

Darman, Richard, on U.S. competitive problems, 170
David Sarnoff Center, 60, 201–203
design
    recognizing flaws, 47–48
    suppliers and, 121, 125
    tools for, 86–87, 173
    see also integrated design
design engineers, 81
dialogue, 150, 151–152
Digital Equipment Corp., 84
discontinuity, 15, 19, 44
dominant design phase, 16–19
downsizing, 147–148, 149
DuPont Medical Products and Imaging Systems Divisions, 64–65, 85, 189–191

Eastman Kodak, 99, 191–194
educational system, 74, 171
engineering, concurrent, 80–82
engineering change syndrome, 75
engineering design education, 74
equipment, 129, 131, 133

evaluating change and risks, 51–54
evolutionary change, 14, 46

Federal Aviation Administration, 95
Federal Products Corp., 84
Ford Motor Co., 84
foreign investment, 176
Foster, Richard, on discontinuity between old and new technologies, 15

Galbraith, John Kenneth, on power of technostructure, 148
Gemini Consulting Survey, 128, 146, 162, 169–185
General Motors, 50
geography, 149–154

Hayes, Robert, on tortoise or hare approach to risk, 44–45
Henderson, Rebecca, study by, with Clark, 17–19

IBM Corporation, 43, 58–59, 107, 116–117, 118, 142
incremental change, 14, 46, 204
industry, *see* U.S. industry, roadblocks to leadership, 1
informal networks, 24, 148, 149
and top management, 24
information, 19, 148
innovation, rate of, 7
integrated design, 36, 47, 71, 80–85
evaluating and improving, 88–91
potential problems in, 84–85
steps in, 87–88
integrated teams, 143–146
integration, 21, 47, 165
of components, 121
and investment timing, 133–135
of operations, 5, 10, 11–12
of research, 61–67
success of, 85
of supplier, 36, 124–128
top management and, 158–159

internal corporate problems, 172
International TechneGroup Incorporated, 97
investments, 36, 129–137
foreign, 176
top management and, 157–158

Japan, 73, 99, 102, 126, 143, 173

Kevlar, 17
Kodak Copy Products Division, 65–66

leading-edge products, 77
lead time, for equipment purchase, 133, 135
learning, 138–154
environment and, 159
and management hierarchy, 148–149
organizational, 138–140
longevity in job, 143

make-or-buy decisions, 113–120, 127
management
and learning, 148–149
stability and continuity in, 140–143
see also top management
manufacturing
management rating of, 180
and product design, 72–73, 80–85
research and, 62–64
manufacturing engineers, 81
manufacturing facility, 90–91
marketing strategies, 39, 42
market needs
performance specifications and, 40, 42
product concept and, 40, 42
materials, in design, 90
middle management, 147
MIT Commission on Industrial Productivity, 169
Morton, Jack, on innovation, 66

National Aeronautics and Space
    Administration (NASA), 92
networks, informal, 148, 149
new products, 5, 157–158
    change in, 45, 47–48
    critical changes in, 52
    risks of, 48–51

organization, 189
    effectiveness of, 140
    learning by, 138–140
    manager and, 159
    for research, 65
organizational chart, 23–24

performance, 40, 42, 160–161
pilot production, 101–102
process, 22
    and product design, 36
process chart, 32
process research, 60
process tools, 114
product concept, and market needs,
    40, 42
product design, 70
    objectives of, 72–73
    problems with American, 73–74
    see also integrated design
product development cycle, 9, 22,
    25–32
    component supplier and, 124
    critical elements of, 35–38
    engineering changes in, 75–80
    impact of technology on, 8–11
    and integration, 21, 61–67
    length of, 2, 4, 9
    management and, 27, 141–142,
        156–163
    problems in, 94, 96
    prototypes in, 109
product development process, 24,
    30–32
    customizing, 33
    success of, 34
product goals, 39
production
    automated, 78–79

building plants, 129
    premature investment and, 132
production workers, 81, 166–167
productivity, 87
product-oriented research, 60
products
    leading-edge, 77
    performance, 7
    selecting alternatives, 42–43
program manager, 32–33
    authority of, 33
prototypes, 36, 47, 92–110, 192
    character of, 100–102
    cycle for, 103–106
    do's and don'ts of using, 106–108
    function of, 102–103
    optimum number of, 97–98
    planning, 108–110
    timing of, 98–100
    use of, 95–97, 197
purchasing department, 81
pure research, 59–60

quality control, 77, 116, 179

raw materials specifications, 59
RCA Consumer Electronics Divi-
    sion, 83
research, 55–69, 187
    amount needed, 67–69
    collaboration with manufactur-
        ing, 62–64
    and product development,
        61–67, 82
    see also applied research
research laboratories, 59, 202
research scientists, 10
resource allocation, 158
revolutionary change, 14, 46
risks, 27, 164
    evaluation methods for, 51–54
    in new products, 48–51
    of premature investments, 131–
        133
    reducing, 135–137
    technological change and, 43–45

Rosenthal, Stephen, industry-university study by, 87

serial approach, to investment timing, 133, 134
simplicity, 90
simulation, 97–98
skills, 22
Stanley Magic-Door, 117–119, 198–200
strategic direction, 39–54
strategic issues, 40–45
  marketing, 39
  top management and, 157–158
success, 4, 140
suppliers, 111–128, 200
  design problems of, 121
  integrating, 36, 112, 124–128
  make-or-buy decisions and, 113–120, 127
  selecting, 120
synergism, 150

teams, 10, 162, 188, 190
  integrated, 143–146
technical foundation, 7–21, 47, 59–61
  weakness in, 57
  see also research
technological change, 19–21, 164, 196
  adjusting to, 12–19
  categories of, 14
  and product development cycle, 8–11
  size of, and risk, 43–45

technology development process, 27, 29–30
technostructure, 148
Tektronix, 83
tests, on prototypes, 109
Texas Instruments, 84
time-based competition, 4
top management, 6, 21, 33, 164
  and critical path, 155
  and informal relationships, 24
  and integration, 158–159
  and investments, 157–158
  performance rating by, 180
  and product cycle, 156–161
  and strategies, 157–158
  and supplier relationship, 127
  views of, 177–183
Traffic Alert and Collision Avoidance System, 95
transistors, 15–16
Trilogy, Ltd., 49–50
Tushman, Michael, analysis of technology change by, with Anderson, 14–15

upward mobility, 140–141
U.S. industry
  academic view of, 171–176
  competitiveness of, 169–185
  problems handicapping, 19
  roadblocks to leadership, 1

Volkswagen, 83

worldwide competition, 13, 57